***The jaws of death hung open,
waiting to grab me . . .***

I found my flashlight on the silty bottom of the lake. I turned around and saw the gator's jaws opened like the gates of hell. Just as the jagged jaws snapped shut, I pushed the flashlight between them. Then I swam like my life depended on it—because it did!

The gator thrashed its tail and sped after me. Its jaws were still held open by the glowing flashlight.

Marty screamed, "Come on, Marshall!"

Mark pulled me in just as the alligator lunged. The reptile's jaws snapped with unbelievable strength. Then the flashlight flew through the air. Mark caught it, and we all knelt in the boat and watched the alligator submerge like a deadly submarine.

WILD AMERICA™

WILD AMERICA™

a novelization by
RON FONTES *and* JUSTINE KORMAN

based on the screenplay by
DAVID MICHAEL WIEGER

JAMES G. ROBINSON PRESENTS A MORGAN CREEK PRODUCTION
IN ASSOCIATION WITH THE STEVE TISCH COMPANY A WILLIAM DEAR FILM JONATHAN TAYLOR THOMAS "WILD AMERICA"
DEVON SAWA SCOTT BAIRSTOW FRANCES FISHER JAMEY SHERIDAN MUSIC BY JOEL McNEELY EDITED BY O. NICHOLAS BROWN
PRODUCTION DESIGNER STEVEN JORDAN DIRECTOR OF PHOTOGRAPHY DAVID BURR EXECUTIVE PRODUCERS GARY BARBER, STEVE TISCH AND BILL TODMAN, JR. WRITTEN BY DAVID MICHAEL WIEGER
PRODUCED BY JAMES G. ROBINSON, IRBY SMITH AND MARK STOUFFER DIRECTED BY WILLIAM DEAR

MORGAN CREEK © 1997 MORGAN CREEK PRODUCTIONS, INC.
ALL RIGHTS RESERVED.

CHAPTER 1

I didn't die. But my whole life flashed before my eyes—and it wasn't much.

In the summer of 1967, I was twelve years old and living on a farm near Fort Smith, Arkansas. That's way over by the Oklahoma border, right on the Arkansas River. It was hot. There wasn't much to do, except too many chores.

My dad—Martin Stouffer, Senior—owned this boring business. He reconditioned old carburetors. Then he trucked the parts to garages all over the country. So he wasn't home very much. And my brothers and I got stuck cleaning the greasy carburetors.

When Marty Senior was home, he ruled! Dad

could be a bit intimidating, down to his stinky cigars and the way he growled when he demanded chicken dinners.

But the guy working for him, Leon, was just the opposite. See, Leon had been in the air force with Dad. They used to fix all kinds of airplanes, then take them up and test them. After the war, Leon followed my dad home. He's worked for him ever since.

Three years ago, Leon's wife left him. That's when the little house behind our shop became Leon's home. We were his family now.

Leon could spend hours staring at the clouds. We used to do that, just lie around seeing stuff in the clouds. And I would dream about flying, like my great horned owl, Leona.

She was a big bird, speckled and spotted, gray and brown with a white tuft like a beard under her curved black beak. Tufts of feathers on either side of her head stuck up like cat ears or horns, which is why they call her species the great horned owl. But the tufts weren't really ears. I liked Leona's serious look and the way she could turn her head completely around.

Leona had big yellow talons that she used like hands. Owls usually eat small mammals, like voles and mice and chipmunks. But we fed her hamburger meat and she liked it well enough. I'm sure she would rather have been winging silently through the night, swooping down on unsuspecting field mice. But she didn't seem to mind our house, and I think she liked me.

Yeah, I know, most families have a dog or a cat— but not the Stouffers! We had all kinds of pets because Mom loved animals. Everybody in town brought wounded critters to our house because they knew Mom would take care of them.

My brothers, Marty Junior and Mark, and I helped her. Our bedroom was a zoo! That summer, we had four puppies and a red fox chasing around a pile of shoes on the floor. A beaver lived in a tub in the corner. An aquarium of frogs held up Marty's beloved copies of Hemingway's *Collected Works*.

Leona liked to read with me. I'd sit on the bed in my old, cracked-leather flight helmet (from World War II, or "the Big One," as Dad always said) with the *Big Book of Airplanes* spread in my lap. And Leona would perch on the headboard and stare at the pages with her big yellow eyes. Her wing was kind of messed up. She'd been with us awhile. But one day, I knew, she was destined to fly.

I wanted to fly, too, but I wasn't so sure about

myself. Mom always said, "Honey, when you're ready, you can fly as far as you want to go, and everything will be just fine." She said it with such a warm, loving glow in her eyes, and such confidence that everything would turn out fine, that I felt better. I felt like I could soar with the eagles. Then it would hit me that Mom wasn't considering my fear of heights.

I guess it's pretty hard to be confident when you have two older brothers like mine. Because of my brothers, I developed a powerful interest in understanding what heaven would be like. But I had a problem with the whole heaven thing. It was on account of my fear of heights. It's the chicken or egg deal. Was I afraid of heights and so my brothers tortured me with them? Or was I afraid of heights *because* they tortured me with them?

It didn't matter. That day, after chasing me through the woods like a wild animal, my brother Marty held me down and Mark tightened the seat belts rigged to a chair. We Stouffers have a gift for mechanical devices. There I was: safety-belted to a cast-iron lawn chair hanging from a thick branch of the big tree beside our swimming pool.

There was a rusty transmission tied to the other end of the rope attached to my chair. The transmission was the heaviest counterweight they could find.

"Don't even think about touching that belt till you hit fifteen," Marty warned. His face loomed over me. I smelled lunch on his breath, sort of the cherry on the sundae of my day.

That seemed like hours ago. Suddenly, the chair swung wildly back and forth in a sickening figure eight as the branch bounced up and down. Mark, with a knife clenched in his teeth, inched along the branch of a tree right next to mine. He flexed his muscles, like he was so cool. But Mark was also just Marty's stooge. There was a pecking order at our house, and I was at the bottom. They called me Zero. My place was somewhere below the chickens. But someday, I swore, this chicken would fly!

With a wild Tarzan-like yell, Mark leaped from his tree. When Mark's bulk landed on the thick branch that supported my dangling prison, everything bobbed and shook. The taut rope hummed and quivered as Mark sawed through it with his hunting knife.

The thing about being scared is, you get more afraid about the future than the present. But when the future is the present, there's no time to be afraid. It's survival time!

The rope parted with a *twang*. I dropped through the air like some kind of circus freak shot from a cannon. The wind whipped through my hair and rushed past my ears. My stomach had time to float up to my chin just before I hit the pool.

My fanatical oldest brother, Marty, filmed it all on his buzzing 8mm movie camera.

There was no time to think. I prayed for a landing that wouldn't hurt too much or involve a cast—'cause then they'd just make a movie about a mummy.

Ka-splash!

I hit the water and started counting: fifteen one-thousand, fourteen one-thousand . . .

I kept calm. I knew what to do. I waited until the chair touched the bottom of the pool before releasing the seat belt.

Marty would be counting: one one-thousand, two one-thousand . . . with his camera focused on the pool. And at exactly four one-thousand . . . *Ka-splooosh!* The cherry bomb Mark had tossed into the water exploded.

I had just gotten my legs free of the ropes entangling them. A rock plunged down. A cherry bomb was taped to it.

I wonder sometimes why I didn't go deaf. Water

amplifies sound. The cherry bomb sounded like a nuclear test. And then six more bombs went off before Marty reached twelve.

Water sprayed everywhere. I popped out of the boiling surface and gulped air at the side of the pool. Marty stepped from behind his camera and pulled me out. I didn't die. Maybe they wanted me to, but I wouldn't give them the satisfaction.

Mark grinned. "Good work, Marshall. You beat my old record by three seconds."

It was better not to show them fear. They liked it too much. I just looked at Mark and kept my face perfectly still. Poker face, Dad called it. I said, "That's great, Mark."

When I squished into the kitchen, Mom was folding laundry. She scolded me for dripping water through the house and added, "If you boys are throwing firecrackers in that pool again, blah, blah, blah . . ."

I just kept my poker face and peeled down to my wet shorts. I had a plan.

After I dried myself off in the bathroom, I took Mark and Marty's toothbrushes and cleaned the toilet with them. Then I put them neatly back in place. I had to smile.

CHAPTER 2

"I'm thinkin' dinosaur," Leon said in his slow Arkansas drawl. Well, we all talked like that, only Leon more so. You didn't grow up in Fort Smith sounding like a TV announcer.

Leon pointed at a cloud with his beer can. He was an old guy, in his forties. He wore a "Buy American" hat and his usual ain't-the-world-incredible grin. He sat on a tractor attached to a trailer loaded with a pair of fifty-five-gallon drums.

I didn't think it was a dinosaur. I corrected him. "That's a rabbit lying down."

Leon studied the cloud, scratched his head a little, mumbled to himself. "Could be a hog head or mebbe a big ol' skunk. Or a turtle? . . ." Leon rambled on, everything from a Chevy bumper to a cow chip coming to his mind.

Leon made a decision. "Naw. Definitely a rabbit lyin' down." He waved his beer can toward Leona. I stroked her soft salt-and-pepper feathers to keep her calm.

"How's her wing comin'?" Leon asked.

"I want to fly with her someday, Leon." I don't know why I said it. It just came over me.

But Leon didn't laugh or anything. He just said, "You will, Marshall." And he finished his beer and said, "Well, I better git my chores done. Yore daddy gits home tomorra."

It was a day we all had on our minds. Any time Dad showed up was a day to remember. I wondered if my brothers were as worried as I was. But the dreaded day came, and they just acted like they always did. Mark had his shirt off, sweating and grunting, pushing his weights in the air. Marty was sprawled on the carpet reading an *Outdoor Life* magazine.

You wouldn't catch them helping Mom wash dishes, which is what she was doing. She stacked cleaned TV dinner tins in the dish rack. Mom saved everything. She and Dad were pretty tight. "Waste not, want not," Dad always said. He had a lot of stuff he said like that. He believed it, too. And believe me, we had to believe it.

"Hey, Mark, check this!" Marty exclaimed. He held up the *Outdoor Life*. "This is a story from some old trapper's journal."

Then he read the article out loud. "And the medicine man said . . . 'In the land of Eagle People, in Northern mountains far into the snow, where trees don't grow, there is a cave filled with a thousand sleeping bears'. . ."

Mark aimed an imaginary rifle and said, "Hit one every time you pull the trigger."

Marty smiled vaguely and kept reading.

"'Up there, the vapors rise from the center of the earth, and the snoring of the bears is like thunder that rumbles through the mountains.'"

There was a rumble all right, but it was Dad's truck. His old but carefully preserved semi rolled down our driveway. I could picture it down to the neatly lettered sign on the cab door: MARTY STOUFFER, FORT SMITH, ARKANSAS. CARBURETORS BOUGHT & SOLD. The air brakes squealed and the engine shut off. It was like a bomb had gone off in the room.

Mark shoved his barbells under the bed. Marty flung the magazine under a couch. They both raced out the back door. They had a lot of chores to make up for!

When Dad got back from the road, he expected certain things. He wasn't a man to argue with, and my brothers were pretty dumb if they thought they could fool him. They couldn't possibly rake the backyard before Dad got in the door.

I heard the kitchen door bang open. I heard his voice—deep but soft. I couldn't make out his words, but I heard Mom say, "They're out back working." Then I heard her say, "Fried chicken."

His heavy boots clumped on the hardwood floor, tracing the path from kitchen to living room. He was close to me. I could smell the thick, sickly sweet smoke of his cigar. I heard his soft, deep voice ask, "Fried chicken and what?"

"Lima beans," Mom answered. "The big canned ones you like, salad, and peach pie for dessert."

"Store bought?" Dad asked. There was something of a subtle menace in it.

But Mom was no pushover. "What do you take me for?" She pretended to be insulted.

Then Dad pinched her and they got to giggling. Mom pushed him away and waved the smoke from her face. "Go clean up. I'll try to stop those boys of yours from working long enough to sit down and eat."

"Chicken," he commanded. And his command was law. Chicken it was.

You know, a family is like a plate of fried chicken. Each piece has its place on the pile. You've got the breasts on the top, then the legs, and finally the scrawny wings and backs on the bottom.

Marty Senior took a breast. Marty Junior also got a breast. And Mark took both legs. I, of course, was left with the scrawny old wings and the bony old backs.

Dad said sternly, "Give your mother one of those legs."

It seemed like the chicken just walked right over to Mom's plate. Mark did not even think about arguing.

Mom took that leg and put it on my plate. She took the backs herself. She always said they were her favorite part. I didn't believe her and loved her all the more for it.

After dinner I went out to the shop. Cicadas sang in the dusky light. Crickets chirped to each other in the secret language of insects. The windows of the house glowed warmly through bare branches and stands of ragged weeds.

Dad's semi and the forklift were parked in the dried grass beside the rusty, corrugated tin walls of the warehouse. Assorted other vehicles dotted the lawn, including a tow truck and various rusty farm machines.

This was Dad's life's work. Carburetors and more carburetors cleaned and oiled and stacked and counted. That's what we did while Dad drove around the country selling his reconditioned auto parts.

But there was something else in that shed, something really special to me and Dad. It was a dream made of canvas and metal and an old rotary engine. The Ryan PT22 was made by the same company that built Lindbergh's *Spirit of St. Louis.* The fuselage was a two-seater, open cockpit. The wings lay over to one side. Dad was going to have to put them on, but he never seemed to find the time.

Skybolt was painted on her side. She'd been lying out in the weeds at the edge of Bobbie Ray Baker's daddy's farm. They sold her to my dad for fifty dollars and a carburetor for their '52 Buick.

I loved to just sit in that plane and dream. I'd be in my pajamas and my flight helmet, gripping the frayed leather control stick and pretending I was Lucky Lindy or Eddie Rickenbacker or Sky King.

Dad was fixing up the *Skybolt* so we could fly together, like he used to. He could fix anything. I knew if I was ever gonna get over my fear of heights and fly, it would be with Dad.

I was hot on the tail of the Red Baron, banking through the clouds and shooting for all I was worth. Then I heard brakes squealing and Hank Williams wailing on the radio. Doors slammed. A door slid up. I slipped down and hid in the cockpit.

Marty wore his Hemingway bush jacket. He and Mark were with their wild-eyed friend D. C. D. C. had another new girlfriend hanging on his arm, an expensive cowboy hat, and his usual cocky attitude. The girl chewed gum and fluttered her eyelashes. She was even worse than Mark's girlfriend, Julie Ann. There were a couple more girls and guys. I didn't want to risk being discovered to see exactly who.

D. C.'s cowboy boots clopped past the *Skybolt*. He made a beeline for the Mud Hog. My brothers had this fat-tired mud buggy with a mutant engine and the words MUD HOG spray-painted on its dirty sides.

D. C. banged on the car and sneered, "You'll never get this piece of junk together by Saturday, Stouffer."

Mark swung like Tarzan on the chain of a motor lift pulley. The chain rattled down the full length of the shop. Mark flipped off in a perfect dismount. He landed right in front of D. C. "Be there and find out, D. C."

Laughing and cutting up, Mark and Marty's gang found places on the old car seats at the back of the shop. A home movie screen glowed in the gloom.

The projector whirred and flickered. And the thin thread of 8mm film slithered from reel to reel in a shiny, slick celluloid stream. I couldn't help myself. I had to watch.

My brothers' friends loved these shows. They had favorite parts they liked to watch over and over. Like when I got blown up. I was in my flight helmet and goggles, standing on a four-by-eight sheet of plywood with a bucket full of cherry bombs underneath. They loved the way the fuse flashed and squirmed. And then I flew up in the air, five, ten, fifteen feet. I kept my cool pretty well. I surfed that plywood. I was hangin' ten. And then I leaned a little too far. The audience cheered every time they saw that.

They cheered again when Marty skied across grass, up a ramp, and through an eight-foot ring of fire. My brothers' audience liked fire. They loved it when Mark tried to fly with his homemade wings powered by Roman candles. He managed one pathetic flap before he crashed to the ground in a fizzling heap.

But I was still the biggest hit. You should have heard them cheer for my slow-motion flight strapped to the lawn chair, followed by the sparkling splash in the pool.

The group had their fun. Then they all went home. Mark and Marty were already asleep when I tiptoed into the bedroom. Leona and I watched the stars for a while. We felt at peace.

Then I heard the roar of a powerful engine. Dad was in the shop working on the *Skybolt*. He wasn't surprised when I joined him. He just asked me to hold the flashlight.

Leona perched on the wing and solemnly watched us with her big yellow eyes. Maybe she understood that these were my wings and they needed fixing, just like hers. I could tell she approved of our efforts.

I loved to work on the plane with Dad. He'd fire questions at me, and I could answer all of them. You pull a throttle back to the moon on your thumbnail. Green is go for your airspeed indicator, with the tachometer at one thousand. Flaps should be to the second notch. I knew my oil temperature gauge from the pressure gauge and the lateral level from the turn-and-bank indicator.

I knew every bolt on that plane, because Dad had told me all that and more. The best part was when he told me about clouds! Dad said, "You slice through 'em like butter. And when you pop out on the other side, all you've got is the bluest sky you can think of."

"Birds get out of the way, right?" I asked. I didn't want to hurt anything.

"They see you coming a mile away," Dad assured me. Then he said, "Go to bed now, squirt. It's late."

I gave him back his flashlight and went to bed. I lay there with my hands behind my head and heard Dad singing in the shop. It wasn't that old bear growl he usually had. It was soft and kind of nice, some silly old song I think was called "Good Ol' Mountain Dew." Most nights, we fell asleep to the sound of his voice singing that song.

CHAPTER
3

"Piece of junk, huh? Well, this piece of junk just kicked your butt, D. C.!" Marty yelled.

Mark leaped from the trunk of the Mud Hog and cut loose with a rebel yell. *Weeeee-haa!* He still clutched his camera to his chest.

The Mud Hog and my brothers were coated with clay. D. C.'s fat-tired Jeep still idled nearby. There was wild cheering from the big crowd of locals in the center of the race track. They'd just finished a hot race that my brothers had won easily.

The track wasn't much to look at. It was a muddy, rutted oval surrounded by a rusted chain-link fence and battered bleachers. The bleachers were so old nobody wanted to sit in them. So they stood in the center at the base of an old tower with smashed windows and peeling paint.

D. C. was mad. He walked right over and grabbed the Mud Hog's rear fender. He lifted it, and the rear wheels cleared the ground. "No wonder you won, Stouffer. My Jeep outweighs this stripped-down crate by an easy five hundred pounds."

Mark sneered. "You're one sorry loser, D. C."

His rival tugged at an old, rusted car hood. D. C. pulled it free of the mud with a sucking sound. He peered through a hole where the hood ornament used to be. "We can race fair, if you drag this behind you"—a wicked grin split his face—"with Zero on it."

Marty may have said, "Don't tell me what to do with my brother." But while he said it, he was tying a rope through that hole in the hood. "Go on, Zero, get on the hood," he said. He tied the other end to the Mud Hog's rear bumper.

Mark thought it was really funny. He climbed back into the trunk and aimed his camera at me as I sat down on the hood.

I was just getting a good grip on the sides when we all heard the sound of dual exhaust. A white '57 Thunderbird convertible pulled up to the track. Sun gleamed on its freshly waxed body.

Two girls stepped out. There was something about them, the way they moved, the clothes they wore. We all knew they were college girls.

"The Stewart sisters!" Mark said, amazed.

"Back from school for the summer," somebody said.

We knew the Stewart sisters, Donna Jo and Tanna. Tanna looked kind of embarrassed by all the attention. But Donna Jo loved it. They were all grown up.

"Well," Julie Ann snipped. "Stuck up."

But Mark had to flirt with Tanna. He flexed his biceps. Julie Ann groaned.

"Let's do it," I said. I just wanted to get it over with. I tightened my helmet and lowered my goggles.

I could hear the engines roar as Marty and D. C. revved up. I got a good lungful of exhaust from the Mud Hog while they waited for the signal. A bottle rocket went off, and they put the pedal to the metal!

The Mud Hog threw big globs of mud on me. The fat tires spun and finally caught. And we were off!

The race track was just a blur as I struggled to stay upright on my makeshift sled. I swung and swerved behind my brothers' racer. I dodged gooey globs of mud.

This wasn't the worst scrape I'd been through. I'd

started believing there was a special guardian angel for little brothers. Trouble was, sometimes he took naps. And he must have been snoozing that day, 'cause the Mud Hog hit a big bump. Then my sled hit the bump and the rope snapped!

I was flying!

I saw the mud several feet below me before I slapped into the soft track and skidded another twenty feet. When I stopped, there wasn't a clean spot on me.

The crowd rushed over to see if I was okay. I peeled off my goggles and asked, "Who won?"

Some people said it was a tie. Some people said D. C.'s grill was out in front. Nobody was sure.

D. C. growled, "Let's go again, Stouffer."

I prayed for my guardian angel to wake up. And that's when Donna Jo Stewart answered my prayer. "No way you'll go again!"

She and Tanna pushed through the crowd and knelt beside me. They gently removed my helmet and tenderly wiped mud from my face.

Tanna scolded my brothers, "You could've killed him!"

"He's fine," Mark said, resenting the attention I was getting from the two gorgeous college girls.

Suddenly Donna Jo turned to Mark and gave him a

dazzling smile. "You guys are great! There's no way we'd see guys doing stuff like this at the university. All the boys do there is study or throw footballs."

Everyone was impressed. Mark and Marty felt pretty good about themselves. They puffed up their chests.

"Takes an imaginative guy to think of something like this," Donna Jo went on. "The kind of guy who considers shooting out streetlights quality entertainment."

Marty didn't like what he was hearing. Mark, of course, didn't get the sarcasm until Donna Jo said, "The kind of guy who doesn't have too many forks in his family tree. Some certifiable redneck idiot."

Something happened to Marty that day. Something really weird. He agreed with Donna Jo. He said what they'd done was stupid—a dumb idea, he called it. I couldn't believe my ears.

I said, "Marty? Do you really think you had a dumb idea?"

He just nodded.

I got my hopes up. Maybe my days as a human cannonball were over! I said, "That's cool, Marty. That's really cool."

Donna Jo was kind of flirting with him now. She said, "Don't be a jerk, Marty. Grow up. And when you do, give us a call."

The Stewart sisters were serious! Tanna and Mark made goo-goo eyes as the girls walked away.

There was a change all right. But I wasn't sure what it was. A couple of days later I got an inkling. We were at Bud's Camera Store dropping off a roll of movie film to be developed. The afternoon sun slanted through the dancing dust motes above the worn wooden floor. Bud's old dog, Blue, was taking his afternoon nap on a chair in the corner.

"I'm afraid to ask what's on this one," Bud said.

But my brothers didn't hear him. They were staring into a glass case. Pure awe lit up Marty's eyes.

In the case, on a bed of black velvet, rested a 16mm Arriflex camera. To my brothers, it looked like the Hope diamond. They took one look at it and decided they wanted it more than anything else in the world.

"That's no home movie camera, boys," Bud said. "That came from Channel 2 in Little Rock."

Old Bud came around the counter. He wiped his hands on his rustling white lab coat. Then he unlocked the display case and took out the Arriflex.

He handed it to Marty, who cradled the camera like a newborn baby. Its multiple lens housing was shielded by a bellows. The back of the camera looked like mouse ears. That's where the film went. And the long tube beside the film casing was a real diopter viewfinder.

"Go on, have a look through it," Bud urged.

Marty carefully raised the viewfinder to his eye. He slowly panned the shop. Then he zoomed in on Blue. Marty jumped. I wondered what was wrong.

Later, Marty told me he thought he saw an African lion jumping right at him. In the shop, he just said very softly, "This could be it, Mark. Our ticket out of here. If we had a camera like this, our stuff would be good enough for TV."

Bud chuckled. "Takes more than a fast car to win a race."

Marty didn't say anything, but there was the beginning of a strange glimmer in his eyes. We should have known then what it meant.

After Marty talked to Mom about the Arriflex, we heard our parents arguing for a long time. We couldn't make out the words, but it was easy to know what they were saying.

Dad would say they didn't have that kind of money, and we'd just be throwing hard-earned money down the drain. He'd give his I-worked-my-fingers-to-the-bone speech, building this business from nothing, giving us a future, and all that.

Dad had certain tracks he played all the time. And you'd think we were poor from the way he talked. Marty said Dad was so tight, anytime he opened his wallet it creaked.

But Mom could be stubborn in her own quiet way. I'm sure she said it was Dad's fault. He'd taught us since we were little that we had to work hard and be our own boss.

Mom wanted to give us the chance to see what we could do. She even threatened to use her Hawaii money. Mom had been saving money for years, dreaming of that trip. Her dressing table was decorated with dozens of Hawaiian postcards.

CHAPTER

4

The next morning, Mom was making breakfast as usual. But there was something in the air—besides bacon smoke.

"What'd he say?" Marty asked eagerly.

"He didn't." That was all Mom said before Dad clumped into the kitchen.

He poured himself a glass of juice and swallowed it in one gulp. Then he turned to Marty and said, "I'll loan you the money with interest. Right now, I've got a truck that needs unloading."

Marty would have done anything to get that camera, and all the stuff that went with it. That was big money! It wasn't just the camera, you see. You had to have a battery belt to run it, and, of course, you needed a hand-held light to make sure your exposure was good. A heavy adjustable tripod with a pan-and-tilt head was as necessary as a 16mm projector. On top of that, film and processing didn't come cheap. Why, 16mm had to be sent halfway across the state to be developed, all the way to Little Rock.

Marty got a Sun Gun. It wasn't very big, and it had a heavy battery pack. But they didn't call it Sun Gun for nothing! It was blinding, even in daylight. I didn't know how they would ever pay Dad back.

The Arriflex camera itself was pretty cool looking, fancy and all. It ran with the quiet whir of pure precision machinery. On account of that, I thought my brothers would start making movies about new things and forget about me. If I'd known what they were going to film next, I'd have volunteered to jump off the Empire State Building.

As it was, I enjoyed our hike through the woods. My brothers had bows slung over their shoulders. Shafts of light pierced the dense stands of hickory, sassafras, and persimmon trees. D. C. tagged along, dressed in full camouflage and carrying a fancy crossbow. He had a quiver full of short crossbow arrows called bolts.

Marty wanted to make a hunting movie. The

battery belt was charged. The heavy tripod was leveled. The Arriflex was loaded with a ten-minute reel of film. Marty fussed with the focus until he got it just right. Everything was running smoothly when Marty flipped on the switch and carefully aimed the camera at a deer in the clearing.

Then he flopped on his belly in the grass beside Mark. They nocked arrows and took aim. D. C. pointed his crossbow when Marty whispered, "Forget it, it's a doe."

"So what?" D. C. asked. He slid his finger into the trigger guard.

Marty shoved the crossbow down so it pointed at the ground. "You want to hunt with us, you hunt fair," he said.

But as my brothers turned to go, D. C. aimed and fired!

The doe had seen him. She turned and jumped. The bolt sank deep into her rump. She fell and screamed.

Mark cursed D. C., who knew he'd messed up. D. C. fumbled with his crossbow, trying to nock another bolt.

Marty grabbed the crossbow and put a hunting knife in D. C.'s hand. "Finish her," he commanded.

D. C. just stared at the bright blade. He was frozen with horror. The big, tough hunter wasn't up to actually killing.

I didn't really blame him. The deer bawled like a baby. It was a terrible sound.

Marty raced to the doe. I covered my ears and closed my eyes. Everything was blessedly quiet. And when I looked up, I saw Marty covered in leaves stuck to the warm blood on his shirt and pants.

D. C. whined, "If he'd a let me shoot when I had the shot, none of this would've happened."

Mark just ignored him and told Marty, "You did the right thing."

The camera was still running.

When the film came back, Marty told us it wasn't exposed right. We knew that wasn't true, but none of us said anything. And one night I heard the whir of a projector. When I saw that Marty wasn't in bed, I sneaked down the hall to the living room.

On the screen, the doe turned majestically toward the camera. The picture zoomed in on her large liquid eyes till they filled the screen. Marty paused the projector. The cooling fan hummed, and for a long time we both looked into the doe's beautiful brown eyes.

Then Marty punched play, and the film snaked through the projector. The eyes still stared at us, and the picture blurred as the arrow sank into the deer. I never wanted to see that look of horrible surprise again in my life.

The doe fell from the frame. Then I saw something in Marty's eyes I'd never seen before: remorse. He relived that kill, and I had to say something. "Marty, you ever figure if he'd have had a camera, he'd have filmed 'em instead of shot 'em?"

"What're you talking about?" Marty grumbled.

"Ernie-Bob Hemingway. Ever figure that?" I asked.

Marty looked thoughtful. "No, I never did."

CHAPTER
5

We had a little time off that afternoon. We took the Mud Hog down to the Arkansas River. We watched the water ripple lazily past and the sun shining on the peaks of Petit Jean and Mount Nebo.

Marty held the Arriflex in his lap, cleaning it with a rag. The way he cleaned that thing, there was no time to get it dirty. But you had to be really careful with a machine like that. Why, if just a piece of a sprocket hole tore off in the camera gate, it would jam the whole thing. So the Arri had to be cleaned like a GI's rifle. Marty told me that about as many times as Dad repeated anything he knew.

Mark was down on the bank skipping rocks across the sparkling water.

"I gotta get out of here," Marty muttered. "The whole time I'm dipping carbs, I'm thinking about what you said, Marshall. Can you believe that?"

I wasn't sure what I'd said, so I just shook my head.

"About Hemingway killing animals," Marty explained. He patted the camera. "I'd like to shoot 'em with this instead."

"Where would you go?" I asked.

Marty waved his arm at the river. But he didn't mean the river. He meant out there somewhere, maybe the Ozark National Forest or the Ouachita.

"First out there, then Africa!" Marty stared off at the horizon like he could will himself onto the Serengeti Plain.

In the silence, we heard birds, crickets, and frogs. I finally managed to say, "What about Mark?"

Marty practically spat. "He'll do whatever Mom and Dad want him to do."

Mark climbed up the bank, grinning.

"Marty says he's leaving town," I said.

Mark's grin dissolved. "Do Mom and Dad know?"

Well, if they didn't know then, they certainly knew later, when Marty talked to Mom and told her he wanted to film rare wildlife of all kinds—birds, mammals, and reptiles. Her face blossomed into a smile of pure joy.

Then we went down to the shop. Dad was on a creeper under the semi working on its engine. He didn't say anything, but we heard his ratchet clicking while Marty explained that he wanted to go on the road and film endangered animals.

See, Marty figured he could make money to pay off the camera by selling the movies he made. The ratchet stopped clicking. Marty said, "Well, I thought you ought to know."

And then the creeper slid from under the truck. Dad had absolutely no expression on his face when he said, "You're not going anywhere."

"And what did you always tell us?" Marty demanded. "Tell the truth, work hard, don't be afraid of anything, and make your own opportunities. You always said, 'If you want to go out and sell something, it better be something other people don't have. That's where you make your killing.' That's why—"

Mark blurted, "Endangered animals, Dad!"

Dad glared at him and said, "Who asked you?"

"I'm going, too," Mark said.

That was news to Marty and me. For a dizzy moment, I imagined a world without big brothers. It was glorious! Just me and Leona in our room and no home movies, no torture, and all the fried chicken I could eat—the good parts!

Then my brothers went on with their pitch. They planned on filming rare American animals—eagles, snakes, and fish; whatever was getting killed off. People wanted to see them before they were all gone. Marty figured all they needed was one hour of film good enough to sell to TV. He intended to stay on the road till he got it.

Dad's eyes hardened. The ratchet spun in his hand. Then he put it in its place on the tool rack. "Mark's still got two years of high school. That gives you till the end of summer. And it leaves me short-handed," he said as he turned to go.

"You dodo hunters make sure you get back in time to do my first oil change," D. C. drawled as he helped Julie Ann climb into the Mud Hog.

Mark and Marty just grinned. They each held a pile of twenties in their hands. Marty tossed the keys to D. C. They wouldn't need the Mud Hog now. But they did need the money.

D. C. drove off. When the whine of the Mud Hog's engine was drowned out by crickets, Marty asked, "Have you seen Zero?"

Mark shook his head.

They shut and locked the shop doors. They didn't realize I was sitting in an old Studebaker. I carefully rolled down the window and watched while Marty took a small book from his back pocket.

He flipped the pages of the U.S. Wildlife Service Red Book. "Check it out. I say we go for the predators. We'll film every endangered predator in America before there aren't any left to film. There's even a list of endangered species: alligators, wolves, grizzly bears. I figure, who wants to pay money to watch fish like a humpback chubb or short-nosed sturgeon? We've got to get shots other people are too afraid to get, dangerous ones!"

"Mom would kill us before she'd let us film a grizzly!" Mark exclaimed.

"She doesn't need to know," Marty said smoothly. That strange light blazed in his eyes.

Mark looked uncertain. Then he came up with an idea of his own. "If we're going after one bear, we might as well film a bunch of 'em. Maybe we'll find that cave of a thousand bears. Nobody else ever found it. If we do, we'll be famous! This whole town can kiss our royal butts!"

Marty grinned. He liked that idea.

"Let's do a blood brothers kind of thing," Mark suggested.

"We are blood brothers," Marty pointed out.

Mark said, "Yeah, I know. I mean let's do

somethin' so when we get to hatin' each other out there, we'll remember that we don't hate each other so much."

They came up with a crazy idea. Marty held a welding torch and slid a brazing rod into the flame. The rod glowed orange in the hissing blue flame. A hot gob of metal dropped to the cement floor, then another and another.

Mark unbuttoned his shirt. It was his turn to do what Marty had already done.

Marty said in a dramatic voice, "This is to gettin' as close as we can to every dangerous thing that flies in the sky, swims in the water, or walks on land."

I don't know what was going on in Mark's mind. He stared at the burning pearls of metal dripping from the rod. Marty lifted the rod to Mark's neck, and a bead fell down Mark's collar. Mark barely winced as the red-hot sphere rolled down his spine and out his pant leg. It was cool when it hit the cement.

Marty flattened the metal ball with his boot. Then he gave the dime-sized hunk of metal to Mark.

"To the cave!" Mark cried.

"The cave!" Marty echoed.

With the flattened balls of brazing iron in the palms of their hands, they slapped a high five. Metal clinked on metal, skin slapped on skin in their new handshake. Only an idiot would want to have a ball of burning metal roll down his back . . . but if they'd asked me, I would have done it in a second.

Leona and I watched them pack their stuff. All my life I'd dreamed of having my own room. And now that it was about to come true, I was miserable.

Leon was worried. He mumbled and grumbled and fussed while he helped Marty and Mark load bags into their truck. They were extra careful with the camera and the other equipment, like the Sun Gun, the little tin cans of film, and the heavy tripod. Mom filled an ice chest with a stack of homemade TV dinners.

Marty looked around. "Where's Marshall?"

Mom said, "Probably at the creek with Leona. He feels bad because he can't go."

"Kick his butt for us, okay?" Marty asked as he climbed behind the wheel.

Mark looked longingly at the shop. But Dad wasn't going to come out to see them off. He was working. And in his opinion, they were off on a fool's errand.

"It's not that he doesn't care," Mom explained. "He's worried about you boys going off on your own."

Leon chimed in, "You boys drive safe. Don't want

to wind up in a fiery car wreck in the middle of nowhere."

That was all they needed to hear.

Marty said, "Okay, let's hit it!" And they started the truck.

They said their good-byes and Leon saluted. Marty slammed into reverse. The tires threw gravel as he backed out of the driveway. Before long, the farm was far behind and the open road lay ahead.

My brothers left a little good-bye at the Dairy Grand in Fort Smith. As the truck raced past the popular drive-in, Mark heaved a lit cherry bomb into the crowd of hot rodders.

"We're out of here, suckers!" Mark screamed as the hot rodders dived for cover. Old D. C. spilled his drink all over himself.

The truck tore down the highway. Soon we passed an interstate sign:

YOU ARE NOW LEAVING ARKANSAS
COME BACK SOON

Mark read from one of his favorite books: *Wild Animal Attacks*. He was having a grand old time: "'Then the crazed mountain lion dragged my screaming baby out of the camp. I ran after it as hard as I could. But when I finally caught up, it had already chewed off her little leg.'"

"Gawd!" Marty actually sounded sick.

"Wait, it gets better," Mark said. Then he continued: "'Blood was everywhere. I threw myself on the beast and started beating it with my fists. It wouldn't let go. Then it turned on me, sunk its teeth into my ear, and ripped it away from my skull. As I began to black out, I saw another mountain lion charging.'"

Well, Lordy, I couldn't take any more. I jumped out of my hiding place in the truck and screamed, "Stop it!"

I could have killed us. Marty was so shocked he nearly wrecked the truck. But why would they be surprised that I stowed away? Who could miss an opportunity like this? After all they'd put me through, I wasn't about to miss their greatest adventure. But they didn't see things my way.

My brothers stopped at the first pay phone they could find. They called Mom.

Marty told her we were just outside Cotulla, Texas. He said they'd put me on a bus for home.

I grabbed the phone away from him and begged. "Mom, you'd go if you were me, wouldn't you?"

There was a pause, and then she said, "Let me talk to Marty."

I could tell by the look on Marty's face that something had changed. It turned out that Mom decided I could go with them for two weeks. Then they could send me home—as long as I was in one piece.

Well, that's what Marty told me later. At the time, he just slammed the receiver down and screamed at me, "You're gonna pay for this!"

And pay I did.

CHAPTER
6

We camped out that night and cooked a good supper over an open fire. The embers floated up to join the stars in the sky. It was great!

Then Mark started reading from his animal-attack book again. This part was all about bears, razor-sharp claws, shattered bones, sharp rocks, and blood. With every word I got more and more scared of the big, dark emptiness around us. Every cricket sounded like a grizzly sneaking toward our camp.

Then Marty threw a rock in the bushes behind me. I couldn't help myself. I screeched, "Stop it, you guys! Can't you read some other book?"

But, no, they were still my brothers. Marty took the book away from Mark and read this part where the bear is swatting somebody around like a broken, bloody doll. I crawled into my sleeping bag and covered my ears.

The next day, we stopped to take a break on a lonely hill. Down below, a glittering stream wound between poplars and boulders. A shadow passed over us.

I looked up and saw a bald eagle swooping down. The magnificent bird's wingspan was even longer than Leona's. The sun gleamed on its brown feathers and the bright white head with its curved yellow beak. The eagle stooped. Strong claws plucked a wriggling salmon from the shining stream.

Marty sprinted for the camera, but the truck door was locked. Marty made a funny noise. The camera was sitting on the front seat. The keys were in the ignition, and the passenger door was locked, too!

The eagle ate its lunch in the crotch of a tree. Marty picked up a rock like he was going to smash a truck window.

Mark stopped him. It was too late anyway. The eagle had finished eating, and as we watched, it spread its wings and soared up into the clouds.

We decided not to take any chances the next time. See, the problem with wildlife photography is that critters aren't cooperative. You'd better be ready when they are.

But Marty had a time-saving idea. We stopped at Stango's Gator Hell. A bullet-riddled sign said:

SIGHTINGS GUARANTEED

Mr. Stango was happily counting our money on the porch of his swamp shack. "Better watch out for that big one over there," he said cheerfully. "Nighttime's when he feeds. Sucker ate my dog in one bite. Then he come after me. I pulled my knife . . ."

Stango slid a big bowie knife out of a ragged leather sheath and slammed the blade into his own thigh! I gasped.

". . . he got my leg, anyway," Stango finished, rapping his big greasy knuckles on his wooden leg.

Stango pushed his face right into mine. "Know what makes 'em the meanest animal alive? Their tail. One solid muscle bigger than your whole body. One whip o' that thang and that gator's out o' the water and its teeth sunk in ya quicker 'n you can spit."

Stango spat. "But that's nothing to what happens next," he said, so ominously that even Marty and Mark looked a bit shook up. "See, it don't want to eat hunks o' you. What it really wants is to drown ya, leave ya in the sun, wait for your flesh to get all soft and tasty, then eat ya real slow."

Stango bared two rows of nasty-looking teeth that would scare a gator. "He only got my leg. And that really made him mad."

I said, "You showed him."

And the swamp man just smiled and nodded.

We climbed into the boat we'd rented and went into the swamp. Thick, fleshy plants hung out over the murky water. Cypress trees poked knobby knees in the path of the boat. Mosquitoes swarmed around our sweaty faces.

"How about we hit New Orleans and have some fun," Mark suggested.

Marty panned the swamp banks. He was dead serious and had that strange light in his eyes. "This trip's not about fun, Mark. Hand me the bait. We gotta get an alligator eating something, otherwise it'll just look like a log."

My brothers turned and looked at me like I'd make great gator bait. "Jump in yourself!" I said.

I guess they figured they had a better chance with a gator than with Mom if anything happened to me. They just laughed.

Marty set the Arriflex on the tripod in the bow of the boat. Mark stuffed a plastic bag with hamburger meat, then poked holes in it. He whipped the bag around his head and flung it.

The bait bag snagged on a branch, dangling a foot over the algae coating the oily water. It was completely useless up there. We couldn't reach it by boat because the tree was behind a dense thicket of fallen logs and tangled plants. The only way to recover the bait was if somebody got in the water. I was worried that I'd be volunteered for the job.

"Toss some more meat," Marty said.

"I used it all," Mark replied sheepishly. He grabbed a string of M-80s and handed it to Marty. "If anything moves while I'm out there, blow it up."

"Don't be crazy," Marty said. "We can come back tomorrow."

Mark glanced up at the darkening sky. Night was fast approaching, and we were losing the light. Mark had made up his mind. Marty knew that look. He took out a lighter while Mark tugged on a pair of rubber waders.

Mark slipped over the side and waded through the mucky waist-deep water. I shone a flashlight on the dim shore and wrapped the flashlight's strap around my wrist to make sure I wouldn't drop it.

Everything was utterly still. The eerie silence was broken only by Mark's sloshing. He picked his way through reeds and branches toward the bait bag. Blood dripped from the raw meat into the rank water.

Mark reached for the bag and disappeared!

The water swirled and churned. Marty frantically paddled the boat to the spot. We didn't see the barrier of logs until it was too late. Wham! The flimsy boat smacked into the water-logged tree. I flew over the bow, past the log, and splash!

I could see Mark in the murky green and yellow water. He was desperately trying to unhook the strap on his waders. They were snagged on an underwater branch.

I couldn't pull him to the surface. I went up and gulped air, took out my pocketknife, and went back after him. I hacked and slashed at the thick rubber strap until it parted.

Mark popped to the surface, coughing and sucking sweet air. I was right beside him as he made for the boat. The flashlight flopped against my arm with each stroke.

We saw Marty light the string of M-80s. He threw them over our heads. I looked back and saw the granddaddy of all gators! It had to be twelve feet of lumpy green-gray skin. Jagged yellow teeth jutted from jaws too small to contain them all. I got a good look at the pink interior of the gaping mouth.

Ka-boom!

The cherry bombs missed. The gator skimmed

behind a log. Mark was already climbing into the boat when my flashlight caught on a submerged branch. I was stupid! I went after it.

I found it on the silty bottom. I turned around and saw the gator's jaws opened like the gates of hell. Just as the jagged jaws snapped shut, I pushed the flashlight between them. Then I swam like my life depended on it—because it did!

The gator thrashed its tail and sped after me. Its jaws were still held open by the glowing flashlight.

Marty screamed, "Come on, Marshall! Come on!"

He threw another string of M-80s.

Ka-boom!

A column of water geysered up and rained down on the boat with a hiss and a spatter. Mark pulled me in as the alligator lunged. The reptile's jaws snapped with unbelievable strength, and the flashlight flew through the air!

Mark caught it. Then we all knelt in the boat and watched the alligator submerge like a deadly submarine.

Mark said to me, "Looks like all your Houdini practice paid off." He chuckled. Suddenly he noticed a bright red line of blood on his butt. "Hey, you cut me!" Then he smiled and said, "Thanks."

I didn't know what to say. I'd never felt so proud in my whole life. I wasn't a zero anymore.

CHAPTER
7

Night had fallen when we got back to Stango's shack. He was hunched on a bucket, drinking whiskey. His loud, drunken laugh echoed over the water as he watched us tie up the battered boat. We put our gear on the dock.

"Thought for sure you fellers would be the big guy's supper tonight," Stango drawled.

"We almost were," Marty said casually.

Stango's big yellow grin grew wider. His smile looked a lot like the gator's. "Ya got lucky. 'Cause all o' a sudden, *splash, chomp!* My buddy Phil could tell you all about that."

"Please, mister. No more stories," I pleaded. I tried to sound cool but couldn't help whining a little.

Stango didn't pay any attention. "Phil and me served in Korea. Kind o' fell in together, me tellin' stories about gator huntin' back home and old Phil full o' tall tales about bears."

Up to now my brothers had been trying to ignore the old swamp rat. But I could feel their interest when he said the word "bears."

"What kind of tall tales about bears?" Marty wondered. The gleam was back, brighter than ever. Marty was a man with a mission.

Stango drawled, "Phil said crazy things. Like about a cave where a bunch o' bears all sleep together, out west somewheres. Some redskin from Window Rock told Phil stories about it. There's no bears around there, that's for sure. That's desert country. Phil's crazy. Came here a couple o' years back looking for some gator-skin boots."

"Where can we find Phil?" Marty asked.

Stango spat and laughed. "He's here in the house."

He led us into the dark den. Stango lit a kerosene lamp, but I wished he hadn't. Mom would've fainted at the mess. I'm not fussy, but Stango's shack was a pigsty. The place looked like the old swamp man had spent years picking through junkyards and whatever drifted in the dirty water, saving each and every "treasure."

We were confused. We saw plenty of filth, but no Phil. Stango waved us farther into the chaos. He yelled, "Phil! Where ye be?"

The lantern's glow passed down a short hall. We followed Stango. He said, "There you are!" And he raised the lantern. The flickering light danced on a swollen-bellied fifteen-foot gator stuffed and nailed to the wall. Light gleamed on the beast's pale ridged belly. Its stubby little legs stuck out at odd angles.

A pair of cowboy boots poked out of the dead gator's mouth. A beaded belt with the word ARIZONA written on it was cinched around the stuffed beast's scaly waist.

I swear Stango's smile looked even crazier. "Phil got more than those gator boots," he cackled. "He got him a whole gator-skin suit!"

I don't ever want to hear a laugh that crazy again. We couldn't drive out of there fast enough. We watched the swamp rush past us, a mossy blur in the moonlight.

Mark said, "Cave's real, Marty. I know we can find it."

"That belt isn't much to go on," Marty said. "And that guy was as crazy as a rabid skunk!"

I just smiled. "Nothing wrong with being a little crazy. Heck, look at us!"

My brothers looked at me like they were ready to throw me out of the truck, so I just shut up and listened.

Mark's voice shook with determination. He had a light in his eyes like the one in Marty's. "We're gonna find those bears and film them and make those dumbbells back home watch it on TV!"

Marty said, "At this rate, it's going to take a year to get enough film for TV." Then he looked at Mark. "But we'll get it!"

They dug out their metal disks and slapped them together. "The cave!" they shouted.

I just sat in the back feeling left out. Nobody said it, but we all knew we had about as good a chance of finding a cave full of bears as finding a dinosaur.

CHAPTER
8

Days blurred into nights and nights into days. The farther west we went, the fewer trees we saw, until the view outside the windshield was a landscape of red dust and bare rock broiling under the Texas sun. We felt like three lonely astronauts traveling on an alien planet.

Somewhere in the endless expanse of the Badlands was our current goal: a Mexican wolf. I helped Mark drag a battered chunk of corrugated siding across the rocky sand. We leaned the metal against a barbed-wire fence.

Then we climbed back in the truck. Marty drove the truck over the metal sheet, using it like a bridge to protect our tires from the sharp fence.

Too bad we didn't notice the sign on the fence:

U.S. GOVERNMENT PROPERTY
KEEP OUT!

We were out in the desert for hours. I didn't think it could get any hotter. Then it did! Marty and Mark fought over a tiny patch of shade that wasn't big enough for even two people to share.

"Move over," Mark griped.

"Forget it. You move over," Marty snapped.

Mark complained, "How come you get the shade? How come you always get whatever you want and I get what's left?"

It was a good question. But Marty didn't answer.

"Everything I wear, you already wore. Everything I do, you already did. I'm tired of it, Marty. I'm tired of always bein' left behind," Mark ranted on.

Marty looked at Mark, who panted with the heat. Sweat poured down his face, but he didn't bother wiping it. Marty's expression softened. He scooted over to share the shade with Mark.

They sat back to back, silent for a moment. Then Marty asked, "So how come you wanted to come along?"

Mark's voice was soft and serious. "Guess I didn't

want to be left behind. Thought it'd be fun."

Marty grinned. "I'm havin' fun. How 'bout you?"

Mark grinned, too. "Yeah. I'm havin' a blast."

He didn't know how true those words were about to be. I'd been scouting around and had found a watering hole. A few scraggly plants decorated its rim. Not far away from it was a boulder the size of a house. There was plenty of shade there, but the animals would see us.

We had the Arriflex set up on its tripod and draped in a beige towel for camouflage. An antelope and her fawn lapped the murky water.

Then I saw something else. I whispered, "You guys!"

Marty and Mark scrambled up rocks to join me. They wiggled on their bellies the last few feet, staying flat to the ground so they wouldn't be visible.

What I'd seen was a wolf, humped and bristling, creeping slowly toward the dainty tan antelope. The wolf's unblinking yellow eyes were fixed on the fawn. The wolf had set its paws down delicately and was ever-so-slowly creeping forward, like it had all the time in the world.

Marty was getting the camera lined up just as the wolf broke into a run. The dark furry mass hurtled across the sand. It looked like the fawn didn't have a chance.

Boom!

Sand and rock shot up like a volcano was being born!

The wolf and the antelopes raced off in opposite directions.

Boooooom!

Clouds of dust and sand swirled into the air. The ground rocked.

"Cool!" Mark said.

Marty gasped, "I don't believe this."

A pair of jets shrieked overhead. Then we saw two more roaring straight at us.

Marty screamed, "Run for that big boulder!"

We sprinted for the shelter of the giant rock, but right before we got there, it exploded! We just hit the deck. They must have been using this area for target practice. Gravel and dirt and chunks of rock fell like lethal rain all around us. The sound of jet engines faded away.

We sighed with relief. But then, I felt something in the ground. It was still shaking! I put my ear to the ground and heard a sound like thunder. The thunder got louder.

Then we saw what made it: hooves—the hooves of hundreds of wild mustangs. A herd of wild horses crazed by the bombs was coming straight at us in a blind stampede!

Marty was up and sprinting. "The truck! Run for it!"

The mustangs splashed through the water hole. Mark grabbed me by my belt and threw me like a sack of flour into the truck. Marty leaped into the driver's seat. The truck's engine sputtered to life. The mustangs were straight ahead of us—and closing!

Mark screamed at Marty to make a U-turn. I heard the tires spinning in the soft sand before they caught and the truck lurched. We drove straight into the herd!

The horses moved around us. All we could see were foaming flanks, clouds of dust, and wildly waving tails and manes. There was no way we could turn around. I thought I'd go deaf from the thunder of all those hooves. My throat was caked with dust. We all coughed and choked.

Marty slammed the truck into reverse. We drove backward and blind with the whinnying herd.

Marty yelled to Mark, "Take the wheel!"

Then he climbed over the seat, grabbed the Arriflex, and poked it out the window. The lens was only inches from a galloping stallion running right alongside our truck. I could see his dilated nostrils and the whites of his wild, rolling eyes.

Then the herd changed direction, and we were left alone, driving backward in a cloud of thick dust.

Mark stopped. The sound of hoofbeats gradually faded into silence. The dust slowly settled. We could see we were in a box canyon. High rock walls surrounded us on three sides. The tan sandstone was streaked with dark minerals. Through a haze of yellow dust still drifting in the air, I thought I saw a bird flying awkwardly along the cliffs. It looked like an owl. It looked like Leona! I had to follow it. I had to know!

The dim shape disappeared into a wide crevice between two big rocks. I crawled into it and found a cave. The vertical walls stood a hundred feet high.

"Whooooo . . . whooo?" I called in the voice of an owl.

The answer was a ruffle of wings.

I moved farther into the dark cavern. A slash of sunlight cut through the darkness. There must have been a hole above. The bright beam fell on a rock face densely carved with ancient petroglyphs.

I wasn't interested in Indian rock writing. I wanted to find the bird, but there was no sound or sign of her. I strained my ears, listening.

"What're you doin', Zero?" Mark asked.

Startled, I spun around. My brothers stared at me like I was nuts. Maybe I was nuts. I didn't want to tell them I thought I saw Leona. So I said, "Nothin'."

But Marty had already spotted the petroglyphs. "Mark, check this out!" he exclaimed.

My brothers were fascinated by the primitive drawings: Armed with bows and arrows, warriors on horseback hunted buffalo. People danced. There were cryptic symbols, like hands or spirals. And in the center of the rock, framed in a huge sunburst, warriors with spears faced a cave filled with bears.

Mark was in awe. "The bear cave!"

Marty didn't say anything. But he whipped a pen out of his pocket. "What have we got to write on?" he asked.

"Nothin'," Mark said.

Well, not nothin' really. They had my skinny, bare white chest. And they copied the petroglyphs from my chin to my belly button. That was bad enough. What was worse was they took me to a ranger station, where they showed their "map" to some Indian kids.

Two boys and a girl sat on a split timber bench. They had cardboard signs: SEE THE INDIAN RUINS $10. The kids wore cowboy hats, bright shirts, and jeans. One of the boys scuffed his worn cowboy boots in the dirt. Their dark eyes glared at us suspiciously out of their coppery faces.

Marty asked, "What does this look like to you?"

They regarded the web of marks on my chest.

"Looks like a skinny white kid to me," the girl said.

The guy next to her added, "Could be Red 46, quarterback bootleg."

His buddy laughed and said, "Hut! Hut!"

The girl covered her bright white teeth and laughed, too. Her dark eyes flashed. They were having a great time at my expense.

Then we heard this old, wrinkly voice say, "Hey yaaa . . ."

The kids stopped laughing. They fell into a respectful silence as an old woman shuffled out of the ranger station. She looked ancient. Every inch of her skin had wrinkles on its wrinkles.

She fixed her cloudy blue eyes on my belly. She squatted down and stared like she was in a trance. Chanting softly, she traced the lines with a finger that was like an old, gnarled twig. The thick yellow nail tickled, but I was afraid to move.

Marty was very polite when he asked, "Ma'am, do you know where we could find this bear cave?"

Her vision stayed on the drawing. She answered in a dreamy, ghostly voice. "Deep in the heart of the winter wind," she quavered. "In the home of our Spirit Father."

Marty squirmed a little. But he wasn't a quitter. "Can you be a little more specific?"

The yellow nail continued to trace the blue pen lines. Her eyes never left my chest, but the thin, hollow voice replied, "In the mountains of shadows, above the elk, below red feather."

Mark looked disappointed. That wasn't exactly on the road map. "Put your shirt on, Marshall," he said.

But Marty had always been the smart one. He persisted, "Wait a minute. It's north of here, right?"

The old woman said, "Beyond the peak of Arapaho, where the winters come early." Then she looked me in the eyes and smiled a toothless smile. Her bony old hand gently caressed my hair.

CHAPTER 9

Marty was pretty smart. He knew the old woman hadn't fed us a lot of mumbo jumbo. He proved it when he opened the map and spread it on the hood of the truck. Marty showed us the Shadow Mountains and north of that the Elk River, and to the south, the Red River plains. And, of course, Arapaho Peak.

That was enough to have us winding up a steep, rocky mountain road. Marty said it was a race between us and extinction, and there wasn't anything that could stop us from getting there first!

I wished that Mark had been extinct, because he ignored the waterfalls, the pine forest, and the high snowy peaks all around us. Instead, he read from that darn animal-attack book again!

Even with my eyes closed and my sweater wrapped around my ears, I could still hear him droning on with some grisly story about a polar bear crunching bones and . . .

"Hey, Zero! What's wrong?" Mark mocked. "It's only a true story."

Marty was different. All he cared about was the film and our equipment. He started getting weird about it. When we camped, he would tie all the stuff to his sleeping bag. Marty lay awake half the night reading the Red Book by flashlight. Every few minutes he would sweep the beam around, making sure all our stuff was still there.

There was something new in Marty's eyes, something kind of crazy. Making the movie meant more to him than anything.

Me? I was looking up at the stars. I asked Marty, "Which do you think there's more of, stars or birds?"

You know what he said? "All we've got is five, maybe seven minutes of good film, Marshall. We need over fifty for a TV show."

I leaned back to look at the stars again. Maybe I was the only one on this trip who could appreciate how beautiful this country was. I wasn't going to waste a minute of it worrying about the equipment.

*   *   *

But the gear was on our minds and on our backs a couple of days later. We were slogging across a high mountain meadow. The sun shone on the snow covering the peaks around us.

Maybe those stories Mark was reading finally penetrated. He was starting to worry about the bear cave. "What if a whole bunch come?"

Marty talked like he was speaking to an idiot. "They're endangered. That means there aren't a whole bunch. Even if we film three of them in a cave, we've scored."

Mark looked doubtful. "And you think they're going to come down and lead us right back to the cave?"

"You got a better idea?" Marty shot back. "The old woman said it was in these mountains. She didn't say where."

I looked around and saw there were an awful lot of mountains. I'd never felt so small in my life. The cool air was scented with pines. A few birds sang.

Marty took a red wooden tube from his back pocket. I wondered what it was.

Marty admired the tube. "This is bacon in a skillet to a bear."

Mark added, "It's the sound of a dying rabbit. Bears can't resist it."

Marty said, "You're right. You do it." He held out the rabbit call.

Mark backed away, scared. "No way!"

Suddenly I had an idea. Mark had spent weeks terrorizing me. Here was the solution! I wasn't stupid. I knew they'd make me do it anyway. At least my way, the awful stories would stop.

I stepped forward. "I'll do it, if you give me the book."

He didn't even argue. Mark handed over the animal-attack book and the dying-rabbit call.

Just a short time later, I stood in the center of the field blowing on the call. The sound it made was shrill and tortured, like someone was doing something terrible to a baby. It made my skin crawl, almost as much as Mark's book.

My brothers had built a leafy blind. They huddled around the Arriflex like they were in love with it. I looked at them, wondering how long they'd make me do this. But I knew in my heart that Marty would make me do it until he got the shot he wanted. It was kind of scary how intense he was. So, as usual, I resigned myself to my fate—bait. I just hoped my guardian angel wasn't on a coffee break.

Marty nodded and pointed behind me. I couldn't hear a thing over the pained squeal of the wooden whistle. I looked around and saw a gawky young animal wobbling on its long, spindly legs out of the woods. It looked a little like a really homely horse.

The animal had a big droopy face and reddish-brown fur. It gazed vaguely around with its soft dark brown eyes.

I stopped blowing the rabbit call and yelled back to my brothers, "Hey, get me with the baby deer!"

I didn't know what I was talking about. It was a moose. I mean, moose are deer, but they're a special kind of deer. One that can really kick butt if you mess with them.

I didn't see mama moose emerge from the shadows. She was a lot bigger than the baby, with a hump on her shoulders. Her shaggy, grayish-brown fur at a distance looked like pine tree bark.

The mama moose made a short grunt. Her calf took a few more shaky steps in my direction.

I heard branches cracking and snapping in the woods. Something huge and dark pushed through the trees: an enormous bull moose! The animal looked like a car on skinny legs. He was nine feet high and ten feet long! A ton or two of fur and muscle supported a rack of antlers that looked like a little forest on his head.

And what a face he had: long and brown, with

snuffing nostrils and mean little eyes up under his twitching ears. His chin was decorated with a scraggly, bristly beard.

Moose are touchy. They don't see very well. And like any parent, they will protect their children.

Stupid me, I wanted to pet the calf. I ignored the cow's snort. And I wasn't real attentive to the way the bull pawed the earth, ripping up strips of grass and clods of dirt with his heavy splayed hoof.

I didn't even think much of the bull's muffled roar: *Ruumphhh!* I started petting the coarse fur of the calf when the bull lowered its antlers and charged!

Mark sprang from behind the blind. He waved his arms, trying to draw the bull's attention. He screamed, "Run, Marshall! Run!"

I may be stupid sometimes, but not all the time. My feet were thinking! And they were thinking, *Get out of here now!*

I pounded dirt with the bull moose right behind me. The earth shook with his mighty footsteps. The throaty huffs of moose breath echoed over the meadow. His breath was worse than Mark's.

Mark yelled, "Marty, help me!"

But Marty was filming. Nothing was going to peel him away from that camera. I could tell, and it chilled me to the bone. Maybe I slowed down in that moment of shock. Bad move. The bull got me.

The big head slammed right into my back. I felt like I'd been hit by a car. It knocked the breath out of me, but in blind panic I grabbed his antlers and hung on for dear life.

The bull reared up and shook me. I slapped against the hard velvet of his rack. I felt like a rag doll at the mercy of an angry brat.

My feet and legs flopped in front of the bull's eyes. He couldn't see, but he didn't care. He was as crazy as Marty! The moose bolted and bucked around the meadow, trying to shake me off so he could kill me. Yeah, well, I could take anything Marty dished out— even this. My fists gripped those fuzzy antlers like my life depended on it. And it did!

I heard Mark scream, "Help me get him, Marty!"

"I'm getting it all," Marty yelled back.

Who *was* this guy?

The moose rocketed over a rise and down a steep slope right into a raging river. *Splash!* I clung to the antlers while the current sucked the huge animal downstream into white water. We bounced off boulders like a basketball at a championship game. Jagged logs jutted from between the big rocks. My hairy companion and I dropped over a six-foot spill into a seething whirlpool of ice water.

Of all the tortures my brothers had put me through, this was the wildest. And it wasn't over yet!

When we smacked into that frigid pool, I let go of the moose. He'd had enough. The huge bull dragged himself onto the rocky bank. In seconds, thanks to camouflage, he vanished magically into the trees.

But there wasn't time to contemplate the wonders of nature. I was turning over and over in the current, catching glimpses of churning water and blue sky, trees and rocks. The current was dragging me toward the roaring gulf of a waterfall. It looked like the end of the world.

I clutched desperately at wet rocks, but they were too slippery. And my hands were so cold, I couldn't feel my fingers. A stick tore my shirt and my skin as my body jammed between a pair of boulders. Water sprayed over me.

Weakly, I groped for an overhanging branch, but I couldn't reach it. The river grabbed me again and yanked me from my crevice. I realized with horror that I was going to go over the falls. I could hear the roar of water cascading over jagged granite. I imagined the falls plunged into piles of rocks and broken trees. This was a lot worse than cherry bombs in the swimming pool.

Then, all of a sudden, a rifle barrel poked in my face!

I grabbed it. At the other end was a big furry figure. Whatever it was must have been incredibly strong.

The rifle lifted me out and flipped me on the bank as easily as a bear would slap a salmon out of the river. I coughed up water and looked at my savior.

I saw a grizzled hunter dressed in furs. He wore a pistol at his side and two big knives in his homemade belt. A very angry expression creased his dirty, bearded face. He cussed like Dad once did when he dropped a tire iron on his foot. I would've been grounded for a century if I'd said any of that. The hairy man said, "That bull were my winter meat. I been followin' it for a week!"

Just then, Mark stumbled down the bank. He pulled me to his chest and hugged me. He was breathing hard. He gasped, "You moron! Are you okay?" Then he turned to the hunter and said, "Thanks, mister."

Marty joined us. He held his precious camera high to protect it. "I got it all on film! Dynamite stuff! Best yet!"

Everyone stared at Marty. His eyes were wild. I'd never known him to look that happy. He was already accepting his Emmy.

Mark was stunned at Marty's lack of concern. "You what?"

"I filmed it, the whole thing. It was incredible!" Marty wore a huge grin on his face. He looked like he was having Christmas, his birthday, and the Fourth of July all at once. Heck, throw in the rest of the holidays for good measure.

I thought Mark was going to punch him. "What is wrong with you? Our brother almost drowned. He almost died!"

Facts had no effect on Marty. He said blandly, "But he didn't. He's okay. Aren't you, Marshall?"

Well, I was okay.

Then Marty looked at the hairy man. "Who're you?"

Boone was a hunter. And even though we'd spoiled his hunt, he shared his campfire with us. The menu was unusual, and I really didn't want to know what kind of meat it was. It was hot, greasy, and good.

But the best part was dessert: I put the hated animal-attack book on a spit. Then I watched with satisfaction as the book sizzled, steamed, then burst into flame.

We gnawed on grilled meat while Boone talked to us. "You ain't seeing berries and bugs and honey. You're seeing snow and cold. Those bears ain't dumb. They're all fat and happy and put up by now."

That was true. It got cold here early. The bears

were probably hibernating already. That wasn't going to stop Marty, though. I could tell by the look in his eye.

"We're looking for a cave," he said.

The hunter wiped his greasy lips. "Sure you are. Gonna walk on in and snap a picture of a sleeping bear. You do that, nobody's ever going to see it—or you, either."

But Marty had even faced down crazy Stango. "It's someplace in these mountains," he persisted. "It's a big cave, a lot of bears sleep in it at once."

Boone looked scornful. "Ain't no such thing. Bears sleep alone."

"It's real, and we're going to find it," Marty insisted, like whatever he wanted had to happen.

"Let's say you do." Boone smiled, showing big strong teeth that looked very white surrounded by his bushy beard. "You ever seen a bear? You never want to, especially when they get waked up. They're so ornery, they'd rip the heart out of their own shadow, if they had one."

Marty had his dander up now. He finished gnawing his bone and snapped it in two. "We'll find that cave and film those bears," he declared. "In time, mister, you'll see it on TV."

The hunter was not impressed. "Ain't got no TV.

But if you boys ever found a cave like that, I'll tell you what I'd see. I'd see three scared boys goin' someplace they got no right to go."

"We're not scared," Marty asserted.

"Then you're stupid!" Boone countered. "You find a place like that, it don't come cheap. Fact is, it'd cost you dearly."

He studied Marty's face in the flickering firelight. Boone's keen eyes took in the light in Marty's. The hunter's tone changed. "Head up to Willing's Peak and talk to Carrie Stokes. She'll tell you all about that."

Boone winked at me. "Keep a good eye on your big brother, son. He's liable to get you all killed. Why, I remember when a big grizzly . . ."

I had to stop him. "Please, mister. No more stories."

CHAPTER 10

I got to stay an extra two weeks. Marty called Mom from a ranger station. He assured her they'd send me back, if they could, but I came in handy. I reassured her that we were being careful and "safety first" was our motto. I'm glad I had my fingers crossed.

Then we headed up to Willing's Peak. The sign said:

ELEVATION 8,734

The air was cold and thin. We had to leave the truck. The snow was deep, and we weren't outfitted for arctic travel.

Mark thought this lady had to be crazy to live up here a zillion miles from everything. Marty just wanted the gear unpacked. He didn't even feel the cold anymore, and he only had one thought—footage.

Mark noticed me shivering. So he gave me his gloves.

The snow crunched under our shoes. Our breath came in little puffs. My feet were getting numb. The cold made my nose drip. Marty's and Mark's faces were as red as mine must have been.

We tromped until we found a neat snow-speckled cabin huddled in a stand of pines. A thin blue stream of smoke snaked from a stone chimney. We passed a barn, and I heard two horses whinnying. I saw bright red geraniums growing in a little greenhouse. The red flowers in the snowy landscape made me think of Christmas.

Marty knocked on the door. Someone moved behind the lace curtains that decorated the heat-fogged windows. Then a pale hand wiped a big clean circle in the fog. I saw a beautiful woman with pale skin, dark hair, and big blue eyes.

The door opened a crack, and we could see one blue eye. This had to be Carrie Stokes. She said, "Go away. I don't take visitors."

There was something of the wild deer in her eye.

Marty hefted the Arriflex—he never let it leave his hands—and put on a big friendly smile. "We're filmmakers, see? We want to film bears, and we're looking for a cave—"

She cut him off. "No caves around here."

"We were told you could help us," Marty went on. There was that gleam again. He wasn't going to leave until he got the shot.

"I'm sorry," she said sadly.

Carrie looked at me. I shivered and wiped my cold nose. I thought maybe if I looked really pathetic she'd let me go inside for a few minutes to see if I still had toes.

"Ma'am, we've come a long ways," Mark spoke up.

"And you're letting the little one freeze," she said. "Come in and warm him up, then you head back down the hill." Carrie stepped aside to let us pass through the door.

Like I said, we thought maybe Carrie Stokes was crazy, living up there all by herself. But when we came into her warm, cozy cabin, we saw why she lived in total isolation. One half of her face was beautiful. The other half was a red, raw mass of old scars. The eyelid on that side drooped. And the corner of her mouth was pulled back in a horrible, tooth-baring grimace.

"I'll go put on some water," she said.

"Did you see her face?" I whispered to Mark. How could he not? She looked like something out of a horror movie. I felt bad for being afraid of her face. This woman had done nothing wrong. She wasn't a monster. But it was hard to get used to that gruesome ruin of a face.

Carrie was very careful to present her good side to us as she poured tea. We chowed down on homemade bread and jam. Logs crackled in the fireplace. The whole cabin smelled like pine.

"Whoever convinced you this cave of bears was something real was just playing with you," Carrie told us.

"But you've heard of it," Marty said. He was on the trail!

"No," Carrie answered. "Ever since my . . . accident, I've heard a lot of old bear tales, but I've never heard anything like that. Bears sleep alone."

I looked into those pained blue eyes, and I didn't believe her. Carrie didn't hold my gaze long. She pointed to a photo on the fireplace mantel. In the frame was a young Carrie with no scars. She stood with a handsome man who had his arms around her waist.

"That was my Judd," she explained. "He never came out of the place I got this." She smiled sadly. "We were to be wed on his birthday, August twentieth. Tomorrow," she said absently. Then she became grim. "I celebrate that alone every year."

"Sorry," Marty said quietly.

"Me, too." Carrie stared into space for a moment. Then she stood up and took a cracked leather flight jacket from a rack. She gave it to me. "Keep it."

We all understood that it was time to go. Carrie helped me into the jacket and zipped it up. Old leather smells really good. I couldn't wait to wear it in the *Skybolt*.

"Go home," Carrie said, almost as if she'd read my thought. "You kids could get hurt bad running around these mountains chasing old bear stories."

We were halfway down the hill when I sidled up to Marty. "She's lying," I said. "She knows where the cave is."

Mark challenged, "How do you know?"

"I just do." Sometimes you know things. I felt like she was trying to protect us, which meant she knew about something dangerous.

Well, somebody should have been protecting us. That old guardian angel must've been asleep again, because our truck had been ransacked. A vent window had been busted in, and everything was gone! Somebody had written THANKS on the dirty windshield. I guess that old griz hunter had been right. We certainly paid a pretty high price to visit Carrie. And we weren't near done paying yet.

Mark's jaw dropped.

"What about the film?" Marty screamed. The fire in his eyes had blazed into something frightening. This wasn't my brother anymore. He was a robot or mad scientist with only one purpose in life.

"Film?" Mark screeched. "Somebody stole our money, sleeping bags, food, everything!"

Marty clawed under the front seat and pulled out a heap of sealed silver cans of exposed film. He sagged with relief into the seat and cradled the flat disks in his lap. His babies made a dull clunking. With one hand, Marty checked the little yellow tapes that sealed each can. His other hand clutched the camera. I could tell he was pleased that he'd carried the Arriflex down to the cabin. I had a feeling Marty was never going to be parted from it again.

"Well, they didn't take everything," Marty sighed.

"We can't eat film," Mark fussed. "We can't sleep in it. It's over!"

I thought Mark had a perfectly reasonable point. My little frostbitten body voted for home. I could practically smell the fried chicken. Even the necks would be good.

I sneezed. "Let's call Mom. She'll send us some money."

"There's no more money to send," Marty said calmly. "We've got to rely on ourselves." The nutty bonfire still flickered in his glazed eyes. Changing Marty's mind was going to be about as easy as changing Dad's.

You have to give Mark points for trying. He grinned nastily. "Sounds like Dad talkin'."

I agreed. Marty even looked like Dad when he glared at Mark. It was the kind of look that meant Dad had the belt out. Somebody had done something wrong, and justice was coming.

I didn't think we needed a fight, so I said, "Dad has money."

Marty said, "Yeah, right. Maybe he could fly it over in a plane himself and drop it off."

"Yeah, maybe he could," I said.

"That's right, Marshall." Mark bit his lip. "Maybe he could." I was a little bit confused, because Mark agreed with me.

Marty scoffed. "Dad's never flown a plane in his life."

What? Marty was crazy! This was proof. He was out of touch with reality.

Mark's voice was low with menace. "Cut it out."

But Marty kept on talking. "Dad was only a mechanic. He's scared to death of heights." My brother turned his wolf's eyes on me. "Just like you, Marshall."

What was he talking about? Dad wasn't scared of anything! Or was he? I'd never actually seen Dad fly.

"I said leave him alone!" Mark breathed huskily. He was still protecting me. But he wasn't denying what Marty said. Could it be that Dad really was chicken?

I didn't believe it. "You're a liar!" I cried. "Dad's flown lots of times, right, Mark?"

Mark didn't answer. My stomach did a flip-flop. Things looked kind of weird or distant, like when you're in shock. I mean, this is what it's like when you adjust your reality. I suddenly knew the truth. I felt it in the pit of my stomach. Dad wasn't the big man I'd been told he was. He was just as scared as me.

Mark said, "Get in the car."

"What's this?" Marty sneered. "You're Marshall's protector? From devil to angel. I must have missed the great transformation."

Mark was barely able to keep his fist at his side. "Shut up," he growled like a bear. I was scared they were going to kill each other. I pictured all those gruesome stories, blood and bones and crunching.

"You don't really want to make films, grease monkey," Marty taunted. "You should go back to the shop, where you belong."

That was it. Mark snapped. He roared and charged Marty like that old bull moose. Marty howled as they both tumbled off the steep snowy embankment, rolling down snow and ice, punching blindly at each other.

They landed hard at the bottom of the hill. Something went crack, like a big stick or maybe a bat breaking after hitting a home run.

Marty was on top of Mark. Mark lay with his leg twisted at a weird angle beneath his body. His face was almost as white as the snow. Mark didn't want to move.

"Jeez, Mark. I'm sorry!" Marty wailed.

Mark winced in pain and choked out, "It wasn't your fault."

You know, it's funny, but right then is when I realized how much they loved each other.

CHAPTER 11

We managed to drag Mark back up to the truck. I've got to give him credit. He didn't cry or make much noise at all. Maybe he really was as tough as Hemingway.

We found the rugged country home of Clancy Pierce, M.D. He was a bearded country doctor who quickly set Mark's broken lower leg in a ankle cast and gave him a shot for the pain. Mark's tense face relaxed.

By that time, Marty had finished talking to Mom. He was smooth. He'd gotten real smooth ever since that gleam lit up his eyes. Marty explained everything to Mom and told her we'd be starting home in the morning.

Dr. Pierce was a kindly man who trusted us to pay his bill by mail. He even threw in a pair of crutches.

As Mark hobbled out of the room, Marty grabbed my shoulder. He said, "Let's go, squirt."

But I didn't budge. Only Dad called me that. I looked my brother square in the eye and said, "Don't ever call me that again."

Mrs. Pierce glanced away from her baby long enough to ask, "Do you boys have a place to sleep tonight?"

"We'll head down the road a bit and sleep in the truck," Marty said cockily.

Where was he getting these weird ideas?

"Bull," Mrs. Pierce said. "You can sleep on the floor in our living room."

That was more like it. The Pierces even fed us breakfast.

While we gobbled second helpings, Mrs. Pierce made a birthday cake for one of her kids. That reminded me of something, but I wasn't sure what. It didn't come to me until we were already on our way home. We were passing a graveyard, and I was playing with the rabbit call. I saw an old lady laying flowers on a grave.

"Stop! Stop the car!" I suddenly shouted.

My brothers glared at me. But Marty pulled over. "What's wrong with you?" he demanded.

"What's today?" I asked.

"Who cares?" Mark grunted.

"It's Judd's birthday," I said. They looked at me blankly. "Carrie's fiancé."

Still the blank look.

"So what?" Mark asked.

"We've got to go back. Turn the car around. He was eaten by bears, right?" I couldn't believe they weren't following me.

"Yeah, so?" Marty drummed his fingers on the wheel.

They could be so dense! I had to explain it to them. "She said he never came out from the place they got attacked. She's going to bring flowers to his grave today. She's going to the cave, you guys. We can follow her."

Lightbulbs went off in their heads. Marty swung the truck around in a U-turn and sped back the way we came.

Smoke still drizzled from the chimney of Carrie Stokes's cabin. I noticed the greenhouse was open, and there wasn't a red geranium in sight. There were booted footprints in the snow.

Carrie didn't answer the door when Mark and Marty knocked. I followed the boot prints to the barn and saw one of the horses was gone.

Hoofprints led behind the barn and up a hill. Despite Mark's broken leg, we followed them. Marty carried the gear. Of course, we couldn't go very fast. I led the way, following the horse tracks before they vanished in the drifting snow.

Wind screamed and clawed at us. Icy fingers cut through our clothes, and snow smacked like glassy buckshot into our stiff faces. The sparkling crystals steamed like smoke from drifts and piles. The wind whooped and howled around the peaks towering above us.

We had to lean way forward just to keep moving against the cruel icy blast. The wind pushed against our chests like a row of defensive linebackers. It sounded like a crowd roaring in the biggest stadium in the world.

Marty helped Mark walk. "Are you sure you're okay?" he asked, his arm wrapped around Mark's shoulders.

"I wouldn't miss this for anything," Mark grunted.

I trekked on, following my instincts, because I could barely see the tracks anymore. Wet snowflakes stung my skin and eyes as I stared into the blank whiteness.

My ears were numb. I'd grown used to the endless shriek of the storm. But above its banshee wail, I heard a horse nickering. The sound led us to a sheltered ravine. The horse was tethered to a pine tree.

We lay on our bellies in the snow and watched Carrie Stokes slowly walk to the black mouth of a cave. Her unscarred hand gently held a bunch of red flowers.

The cavern was fanged with long icicles. As she entered the darkness, Carrie's horse nervously bucked and snorted.

Marty whispered, "That horse smells the bears."

Carrie tenderly set the red geraniums in the snow just outside the cave. She bowed her head. In a little bit, she slowly turned and walked to her horse. We watched her ride away. Then, as quietly as we could, we climbed down the steep sides of the ravine.

Carrie stopped on a ridge in the distance. She just stayed there. The horse and rider looked like sculptures. Maybe she was praying or crying—or both. We just hoped she didn't see us.

The wind was at our backs like a big freezing hand pushing us into the mouth of the cave. We stepped over the flowers carefully.

At least the howling wind didn't reach into the cave's mysterious depths. We felt instantly warmer. Then we realized that it was much too warm.

Instead of the wind, we heard a steady hissing and a sound like oatmeal bubbling in a pot. There was a bad smell. A really bad smell.

I flicked on my flashlight and swept its beam around the cavern. Sulfurous thermals spewed steam from yellow crevices in the walls. Hot mud bubbled in little craters.

We had to cover our noses, but we pressed on. We came around a corner and heard a new sound. It wasn't hissing steam, and it wasn't the blop, blop, blop of the hot springs. No, it was like a baby's rattle, not one but two or three—or maybe a dozen—and then a lot more than a dozen. And then I turned my flashlight to the chamber ahead . . .

Rattlesnakes! Hundreds of writhing, creeping, wiggling, hissing, and, above all, rattling reptiles. Forked tongues flickered as they smelled the air. Beady yellow eyes gleamed in the flashlight's beam. It was like the very soil was made of long, fleshy patterned tubes wriggling like maggots.

I was sure it was all over then. I thought my heart had stopped. I forgot how to breathe. They must have been in the caverns for the warmth. I realize that now. But at the time, I wondered if we'd done the smartest thing by violating the grave of Carrie Stokes's fiancé.

"Don't move!" Marty whispered.

Like he needed to. I was frozen like a Popsicle in the hot caverns. My legs were pillars of ice.

"Timber rattlers," Marty explained. "The heat must draw them in here."

Thanks for the nature lesson, I thought. *Just get us out of here alive!*

"We're not gettin' past 'em," Mark said grimly.

Marty's crazy eyes glanced over his shoulder. He smiled the cocky smile that had preceded so many past tortures. "Sure we will. We'll walk right over 'em."

I thought that was the dumbest thing I'd ever heard. And I wondered if they planned to use me as a sort of human bridge. I suddenly remembered riding on that car hood behind the Mud Hog. And the time in the chair. And air-surfing plywood. And so many other of Marty's deranged schemes that I thought my life was flashing before my eyes—not a pretty picture.

And yet, I had survived all those crazy stunts. Marty was going to finish the movie. He would move heaven and earth to finish the film. What were a few thousand crummy snakes?

I've got to give him credit. Marty had one heck of an idea. We used our jackets to scoop snow from outside. And we dumped a frozen white path across the cave of serpents.

I could feel them wiggle under my shoes. But the cave was warm, and the snow started melting. Snakes popped up like lethal jack-in-the-boxes. We hot-stepped the rest of the way.

Then steam whooshed from a vent. My nerves were shot. I jumped! And I almost stepped on a six-foot rattler. But Marty grabbed me just in time. He did care. But no, he held me up to his face and whispered, "The snake bites you, you scream. The bears wake up, we all die. Got it?"

The horrible thing was: I did!

And if the bears didn't kill me, my brother with the crazy eyes would. Marty set me down. "Watch where you're going."

By now the snow was totally melting, and we ran across the rest of the snakes. I tried not to think about how we would get out—if ever.

We were in another cavern. My flashlight beam only reached about twenty feet. The beam barely made a dent in the darkness. The cavern had to be enormous. We could get lost forever in here!

This was ridiculous. I said, "You guys, we don't even know the bears are back there."

"They're there," Marty the madman crooned in his strangely calm voice. "They're sleeping like babies."

Mark muttered, "Let's just hope they stay that way."

We crept forward. I saw big round shapes like boulders scattered across the vast cavern floor. I could have sworn they were bears.

Mark reassured me they were just big rocks. But I said, "Listen."

We stopped. You could still hear a few rattlesnakes and the whoosh and pop of the hot springs. But there was another sound, deep and rhythmic.

"It's nothing," Marty said.

But he was crazy. I knew I was hearing something. I was scared! I told him, "It's something."

I looked to Mark for reassurance. He just said, "Come on." Mark and Marty walked into the darkness.

I had a choice between snakes and the unknown. I knew one thing: I didn't want to be left alone. So I followed my brothers.

As we walked on, the rhythmic sound grew louder. We couldn't see anything. The mouth of the cave was far behind us. My flashlight was a puny thing. All we saw in its beam were the big round boulders. And my instincts told me they weren't boulders.

I said softly, "I know what the sound is."

Marty shushed me. And the sound stopped!

Then it started again. I knew what it was all right— snoring, the sound of hundreds of face-tearing bears snoring all at once. I said so.

Marty shushed me again. They didn't believe me. Then one of the boulders moved. Less than twenty feet away was a big fat mound of dark, glossy fur.

"My God!" Marty said in a funny voice.

"Marshall, give me the light," Mark commanded. He swept the beam onto another sleeping bear, and another, and another. They were all around us. My worst nightmare had come true.

Marty fumbled with his backpack and pulled out a hand-held light. Then he slapped the Sun Gun into Mark's hand. "Hold this. Get ready to turn it on."

Marty had the Arriflex pressed to his eye and his finger on the switch. I heard the whine of the tiny electric motors and Marty said, "Hit it!"

With a dull *pop* the Sun Gun cast a hot white light on the sleeping bears. Marty whispered, "This is it, Mark! The jackpot!"

I prayed. I went right over the guardian angel's head, right to the Big Guy. And I hoped He heard me because I heard—we all heard—a deep growl of pure hatred. It shook the cavern. I felt it in my chest.

We swung around to see twelve towering feet of angry furry muscle. A huge bear reared up on its stumpy legs. The bear's tiny eyes blinked against the Sun Gun's glare. Giant jaws bared fangs slick with drool.

Marty kept filming. Mark hooked a hand in Marty's belt and limped backward as quickly as he could.

Then another bear got up. I could tell where this was going. More and more heads rose and tiny ears twitched. Beady eyes looked in the direction of the whirring camera.

I stood perfectly still, with my arms at my sides, and I did the craziest of all things: I started to sing. My voice cracked with fear, but I got out the words of the song.

The bears stopped and slowly settled back on their haunches as I serenaded them with "That Good Ol' Mountain Dew," just the way Dad was singing it in the shop what seemed like a long time ago.

Mark was amazed. It worked! The bears were calming down. Some even began to look drowsy.

I kept singing, and the camera whirred. Something wet dripped on me. I saw droplets of condensation falling through the Sun Gun's beam. Water sizzled on the hot housing surrounding the bulb.

Then something went *splat* on Mark's head. He reached up. This wasn't water. It was sticky and white, and it smelled terrible.

Mark pointed the Sun Gun straight up. The ceiling was moving. No, it wasn't the ceiling at all, but thousands of bats!

They dropped from above in a fluttering, squeaking swarm. Leathery wings flapped in the bats' frantic escape from the terrible bright light.

The bears were annoyed. Once again, their nap had been spoiled, and the concert was over.

Amid furious roars and swinging claws, Mark shouted, "We gotta get out of here!"

A claw smacked the Arriflex. The camera flew from Marty's grip and clattered to the cavern floor. The film door swung open and film unspooled into the mud.

Marty could hardly breathe. "The film!"

"Forget it!" Mark barked.

All I could see were fangs and bloodshot eyes, and claws as big as ten-penny nails. There was fur, lots of fur.

Marty managed to grab the camera and the film.

Mark yanked Marty's arm. "It's over! Forget it."

The camera dropped again as Mark struggled to drag Marty to safety.

But there was no safety. Hordes of bears blocked the one exit. We could only back against the rear of the cave. We were trapped!

My flashlight was fading, so I could see a faint blue light shining through a narrow crack in the stone. The crack was too small for my brothers. But I could fit in there.

I tossed my flashlight to Marty. Then I crawled for the camera. The big bear standing beside it didn't even notice me. I looped the camera strap around my neck and fished the rabbit call from my pocket. The simulated death cry echoed in the cave.

That got the bears' attention. Of course, the biggest one had to come right after me. But I had a plan, and I scuttled into that cranny. "They can't get me here," I yelled to my brothers. "You guys go!"

I had to open my big mouth. A massive claw slashed at me, tearing a fist-sized chunk off the soft limestone wall. I backed farther away. I gave him another dose of the rabbit call.

The bear didn't like that. He was mad! He clawed and tore at the rock, trying to get at me. And I kept blowing the rabbit call until I saw that all the bears had forgotten my brothers. But I could tell by their faces that Marty and Mark didn't want to leave me.

"I've got a way out!" I shouted. "Go!"

The claws were getting closer. I kept backing deeper into the crevice. But the big bear had enlarged the hole enough to squeeze in after me.

I don't know how I did it, but I turned around. I got on my hands and knees and I crawled for the blue light. I could have gotten an Olympic medal, if they gave 'em for crawling. The Arriflex swung on its strap, banging against the damp stone sides of the tunnel.

I heard the big bear behind me, still digging and clawing. I thought I could feel his hot breath on my heels.

The tunnel got even more narrow. I had to turn sideways, hold the camera in one hand, and sort of slither like a snake. But just ten feet away was blue heaven—a plate of snow and the sun shining through it.

I was wrong. It wasn't snow. It was solid ice: slick, rock-hard, and unforgiving. I banged on it with my fists, but I might as well have tried to smash a mountain.

The bear was scraping away behind me.

If my fists weren't strong enough, I figured I could kick the ice until it broke. So I hammered away, trying not to look at the shaggy shape behind me. Chips of rock sprayed and clattered under the beast's claws.

Then the ice broke! My foot shot out into the howling wind. I forced my body through the little hole I'd made. I slid down a slope with the Arriflex in my arms. I didn't stop rolling until I plopped at my brothers' feet. They looked surprised.

"I got the camera!" I announced.

Marty hugged me. "Who cares?"

The mad light had gone out of his eyes. My brother was back—and so was the big bear!

The furry brute roared! We saw an enormous paw reach through my emergency exit. But the frustrated beast was too big for the hole.

Marty hugged me tighter. And Mark hugged us both.

CHAPTER
12

I rode up front all the way home. I even got to drive, because of Mark's foot. I was Mr. Cool.

I wasn't driving a truck. I was flying the *Skybolt*. I tapped the dead gas gauge. The needle jumped to life.

"Green is go," I said. "Tachometer one thousand." I pulled on the cigarette lighter nice and slow, priming my rotary engine.

"Airspeed twenty knots," I announced as I shifted into a barrel roll. The steering wheel turned, and the truck swerved.

"Hey!" Marty shouted. He'd been sleeping with his feet out the window.

But I'd lost control. How could I have been so cocky?

I cranked the wheel, but the front end locked! We skidded sideways off the road. The truck slammed into a sign. *Ka-thump!* The sign landed face up on the hood:

WELCOME TO FORT SMITH

"Nice drivin', Zero," Marty remarked.

Just like that. One minute I save him from getting torn to shreds by raging bears. The next minute I'm back to zero.

We had to call Dad. He and Leon brought the tow truck. We scrambled onto the tow-truck bed. Our feet dangled over the back. After weeks of riding in the truck, it was weird to suddenly be looking back at our battered steed.

If there was a way home without passing the Dairy Grand, I'm sure Dad would have taken it. But there wasn't. The brightly lit burger joint was busy. Loud music blared from hot-rod radios.

To top it off, we had to stop at a red light. So we got a good look at D. C. and Julie Ann snuggled up tight in the newly painted Mud Hog. And D. C. saw us. He and his hot-rod pals hooted and taunted us.

"Just in time to change my oil, Stouffer!" D. C. whooped. "Find any dodos?"

He was a dodo, if you asked me. I just wished he was extinct.

Leon and Dad ignored the shouts.

"Time to trade that camera in for a dipstick," somebody yelled.

"Pretty short three months, Stouffer," another voice chimed in.

Fortunately, the light turned green. Marty drooped with humiliation.

"Ignore those idiots," I said.

Then we were passing the city limits on the other side of town on the way out to our farm. The town lights dropped away behind us. Soon we were cruising along by the light of the moon.

We got home. Mom was there with hugs and hot apple pie. Dad just lit a cigar.

"We'll pay you back," Marty told him.

Dad said, "You'll work it off." He puffed on his cigar. "Now that you've got that out of your system," he added.

Marty looked away to stare outside.

I ran down the hall to our bedroom. How could I forget Leona? My heart raced with excitement at the thought of seeing the owl. But all I found was an empty perch: no water dish, no food, not even a feather.

Mom's voice came from behind me. "She got strong enough to fly away. She was a wild bird, Marshall. She didn't belong here."

I held back the tears until after everyone else went to bed. Then I went out in the moonlight and called to Leona. But I saw no sign of her. I did see light in the shop. And inside the shop was the *Skybolt*. The wings were on. The fabric was taut. All the metal shone with polish. She was the most beautiful thing I'd ever seen.

The next day, Marty and Mark were making good on their promise. They sat by a twisted pile of greasy carburetors and silently sorted them. As usual, Leon rolled his handcart around the shop.

I sat in the *Skybolt*. I wore my flight helmet and the jacket Carrie Stokes had given me.

Dad strolled into the shop. "I'm hauling a load up to Rochester," he announced. "You boys have got plenty to keep you busy."

When he turned to go, Marty yelled, "You ought to take Mark with you. He's the one you'll be leaving this gold mine to." Marty almost spit the words.

Dad stopped. Then he walked up to Marty. "Since when are you too good for what we do for a living?"

Muscles rolled in Marty's jaw. They locked eyes. But Marty couldn't say anything. Dad continued in a quiet voice. "Because if you're too good for this business, you're too good for the money it made, too good for the clothes you're wearing, the food in your belly, your new, busted camera."

Marty was silent.

"You too good for all that?" Dad repeated.

Both of them were angry and confused. They didn't know what to do or say next. I sure didn't want to see them fight, so I asked, "Do you really know how to fly a plane, Dad?"

Nobody wanted to answer. I couldn't take it anymore. Leona was gone, and it looked like they'd been lying to me my whole life. I jumped out of the plane. I climbed on my bike and pedaled away. The road blurred through my tears.

I heard Dad's semi pull out, but I kept pumping at the pedals. I didn't stop until I got to my favorite railroad trestle, the one over a pond.

I jumped off my bike and scooped up some rocks, pitching them into the pond. I liked the way the water exploded around the rocks. It made me think of the M-80s in the swimming pool. Suddenly, that seemed like a far distant, carefree time.

Dad's truck rumbled on the road nearby and drove away.

I was angry at Dad, and that made me feel sick inside.

When I got back home, Mom had a present for all of us. I was still feeling sick, but I didn't want to spoil her fun.

So I tore open the brightly wrapped package. In the box was a roll of tickets, bags of unpopped popcorn, and a bundle of posters announcing the screening of our movie.

Mom was very excited. "Bud said the film should be back by Thursday night."

Mark looked in the box, saw a key, and picked it up. He raised an eyebrow at Mom.

She smiled. "The school gym. I rented it for Friday night."

"We didn't get enough film, Mom," Marty whined. "It'll never make a real show."

"If you boys think what you've got is any good, show it," Mom said pleasantly. "If not, we'll play basketball."

None of us wanted to ask Mom where she got the money. We knew she'd say her Hawaii trip could wait.

A lot of things could wait. Dad's truck jackknifed, and he was taken to the hospital at Fort Chaffee. He was wrapped in bandages and hung in traction.

I felt very sad. The truck was totaled. The load was destroyed. The whole thing had been on fire. Dad was lucky to get out alive.

Mom told Dad the bad news. He said, "Tell Leon you want the connecting rods. They're in the back shed. I saved them for a rainy day. With the doctor bills and everything else, it'll be raining pretty good. There's a guy in Pittsburgh who'll give you seventy-five cents apiece for them if they're put together." Dad looked at us. "I saved parts, not cash. We're gonna need some money."

"Your father needs rest," Mom said. "We have work to do."

Dad asked Marty to stay a bit. Marty told me later, Dad said he was counting on him. "This could break us," he said. That was heavy. I'd never even considered that something might come up that Dad couldn't handle.

We worked, sweaty, grease-stained, and exhausted, for what seemed like years. We sorted through an endless pile of greasy metal parts. We tried to match caps with rods, with about three misses for every hit. And if we found a cap that fit the rod, we pounded it on and started all over again. Even Mom had to help.

The work was mindless and boring, but you couldn't daydream because you had to pay attention. It was horrible.

And just when we thought we'd made a dent in one pile, Leon would drive in with the forklift to deposit another crateful. They were blackened and rusted and had to be cleaned.

Leon looked at our oil-streaked faces. He picked up a carburetor and scrubbed it with a brush. Leon tried to sound cheerful. "Lot of folks going to the big show tomorrow."

I heard Marty mumble, "Yeah, right. But I'm not goin'."

"What do you mean you're not going?" Mark was as surprised as the rest of us.

"What's the point?" Marty asked bitterly. "It's no good. You want to go make a fool out of yourself, be my guest."

Mom frowned. She stood up suddenly and straightened her aching back. She was fed up. Mom was fed up! "This isn't easy for me, either," she snapped. She threw down the rod she was holding. It dropped into the crate with a loud clang. Then she walked out.

"You guys? Know what the great thing about these rods is?" I asked. "They don't chase you."

My brothers ignored me and went back to work. But I was going to needle 'em. It was their turn to get tortured.

"No, I mean it," I continued. "They just sit there in front of you. You should have filmed these. At least they'd be in focus, not like most of the stuff you shoot." I couldn't resist adding, "Especially that wolf."

Marty banged a cap on a rod. "It's in focus."

"Yeah, maybe you got lucky on the wolf," I conceded. Then I got serious. "You know, you're better at building carbs, and it's good you're stickin' with it. I think you're right. The movie would have been a loser anyway."

Marty stopped hammering. He was disgusted. "You sound just like Dad."

I got up and walked out.

CHAPTER

13

I felt like I didn't have a friend in the world. I missed Leona something fierce. I couldn't sleep. I flung off the covers, got up out of bed, and went to the window. I leaned against the sill and looked out at the stars. There was a gentle flapping of wings. Something white flashed across the sky and landed in a big tree in the yard.

I couldn't see it very clearly. It was too far away. It was just a shimmer of light, but I called to it.

And when I did, the ghostly bird floated up from the branch and—for just an instant—I saw it was Leona. Her square-tipped pale wings were silhouetted against the black sky. In that instant, I knew what I had to do. I got dressed with deliberation.

The sky was getting light. I backed the puttering tractor up the shop driveway. I tied a rope to the hitch and ran the rope into the shop.

When I came back out, I climbed aboard the tractor. I popped the clutch. The big wheels started rolling. The rope snapped taut, and slowly and majestically the Ryan PT22 rolled forward and cleared the shop's doors. The *Skybolt* was parked on the dirt road near our house.

I didn't have much time. So I wired six-inch wooden blocks to the floor pedals of the plane. Give me a break. I was just a kid. My legs were short.

I climbed into the cockpit. I took a final look at my home. I might never see it again.

I flipped the master switch, pulled the prime knob, and opened the throttle like I had done so many times in the garage. I reminded myself that the throttle came back to the moon on my nail.

Then I pushed the starter button. A seven-hundred-horsepower engine makes a lot of noise. Birds flew up from the trees. The engine sputtered and coughed. The propeller started spinning faster and faster, until it was a flashing blur.

From the corner of my eye, I saw the aluminum door of Leon's trailer bang open. His hair was sticking every which way, and he was trying to pull on his pants as he ran toward the *Skybolt*.

The tachometer was climbing steadily: 400, 600, 1,000.

I eased my toes off the brakes. The plane started to roll faster and faster. The *Skybolt* fishtailed a little as I taxied down the road.

The needle of the tachometer dial moved from yellow to green. Green was go! I rammed the stick forward and counted under my breath: one one-thousand, two one-thousand . . .

The plane's nose dipped forward a little. I felt the rear wheel rise.

Leon loped up the road and leaped onto the plane's wing just as I yanked the stick back with my left hand. My right hand pulled the throttle. The *Skybolt* jerked, and Leon tumbled into the backseat headfirst.

He screamed, "Marshall!"

I saw his feet kicking in the air and yelled, "Hang on, Leon!"

The wheels left the ground, and we were airborne—just barely. The wings wobbled drunkenly from side to side as I tried to find level. A line of trees fifty yards away was closing on us fast!

"Marshall, what are you doin'?" Leon bellowed.

Well, that was dumb. I answered him. "Flyin', Leon."

Leon's eyes popped as he noticed the approaching trees. He squinched his eyes shut. "Well, fly higher!"

Cattle scattered as we left the dirt road and bounced across an open field. Then the plane slowly rose, almost like a tired old man going upstairs. We just missed the tree line. We greeted the sun as it cleared the horizon in a glorious burst of shining rays.

I leveled out and climbed toward the clouds. Over the steady drone of the prop, Leon bellowed, "You know what you're doin', right?"

I wasn't going to let him know I was afraid. I scanned the controls and said, "Sure. I've done this in my dreams a million times."

Leon didn't answer. I glanced back and saw him with his eyes clenched, lips tight, and his shoulders pressed up to his ears. He looked like a cartoon of someone scared.

I pointed to a cloud. I figured I could calm him down when I said, "I see a hound dog sittin'. How about you?"

Leon didn't even open his eyes. His teeth chattered. "Yeah, definitely a hound dog sittin'."

We hadn't crashed yet, so I was doing pretty good. I got the plane level, and we were flying straight toward that old hound dog in the sky.

I'd never seen anything so blue. Down below was Fort Smith laid out like a tiny toy town. I saw churches and a baseball diamond. The sun sparkled on swimming pools and hundreds of dewy lawns.

Leon relaxed. His timid smile grew bigger the farther we sailed. He waved an arm at the hospital way off in the distance. "Your daddy would sure love to see this," Leon shouted.

I just grinned. "He's gonna."

My sneakers worked the pedals.

I found out later that Marty, Mark, and Mom had also heard the engine. And even as the *Skybolt* banked toward the hospital, Mom and my brothers were following in her car. And Mom was mad!

Marty told me he asked her, "What're you gonna do, Mom, ground him?"

She said, "Very funny." But Marty said she wasn't laughing.

I was going to finally find out what flying through a cloud was like. The big fluffy white mass loomed in front of us.

Suddenly, one of my pedal blocks slipped loose and bumped on the floorboard. I stretched my foot down, but I couldn't even skim the pedal. I tried to keep my head up to see above the dash, but my arms were too short to fix the pedal at the same time.

I said, "Steer, Leon!"

"I don't know how!" he bawled.

"Just keep the stick from wiggling," I yelled above the noise. I ducked down to the floorboards and repaired the pedal. I lashed the wire tighter around it. Just then, the *Skybolt* entered the cloud.

Leon wasn't much of a pilot, I can tell you. The wings wobbled, and we were dropping fast. I got knocked around pretty good before I finished tying down the block. I had to fight my way back into my seat.

But I grabbed the stick and was in control again. I had to laugh. I was flying!

Leon was still screaming, but I was laughing. Then Leon was quiet. I turned around and saw him sliding down inside the seat compartment. He'd fainted.

Before I knew it, the hospital was getting bigger and bigger. I tried to remember which side Dad's room was on. I circled the building and I saw him standing at the window. He was squinting in the bright sun. I smiled and waved. I was flying!

Marty said he told Mom I was waving to Dad. He said she thought I was waving to all of them.

But I still didn't know they were watching me. I knew Dad saw me. That was the important thing.

I leaned back and asked, "Leon, did you see the look on my dad's face?"

Leon didn't answer. I turned to see if he'd woken up.

Then I noticed that Leona was flying behind the plane! Her wings beat the air as she caught up to the *Skybolt*. She flew right alongside the cockpit. I wanted Leon to see this. "Wake up!"

But in Leon's place, I saw my dad. The wind whipped through his hair. He had a calm, confident look in his eye, like a heroic fighter pilot.

Maybe because I'd dreamed it so much, I wasn't very afraid. Or maybe because I felt that Dad was with me. I don't know. But I do know we sliced through the clouds like butter, just the way Dad said we would. It was like glowing fog inside. And when we burst through the other side into the bright daylight, the blue sky was dazzling. Even Leon was thrilled.

Well, it couldn't last forever. So, a few minutes later, I was looking down my "runway," the stretch of level field and dirt road near our house.

I slowly eased the stick forward. The nose dropped. The plane went lower and lower. The ground rose up to meet me, going faster and faster as we dropped to thirty feet, twenty feet, ten feet. The landing gear kissed the earth. Rubber tires squealed. I dropped flaps, but I was still going too fast! The plane careened across the grass.

I killed the master switch. I pushed the throttle forward. The plane still barely slowed down.

I whipped past Mom's car, which was just pulling into the field. I was bouncing over the uneven ground, straight toward the shop!

The *Skybolt* leaped one last muddy bump and thumped down hard. I rolled straight through the open shop doors. Less than a foot from Dad's big workbench, the propeller made one last turn and stopped. You can bet I thanked my guardian angel. It sounded like Leon was thanking his—and everybody else's.

I jumped from the cockpit. Mom's car squealed to a stop outside. Mom, Marty, and Mark piled out. I casually flipped up my goggles and smiled. "Morning, everybody!"

Mom's face was dark as a thunderstorm. "Just thought you'd take her up for a spin, huh?"

I just nodded and grinned. I felt great. I was still flying!

"Why?" Mom asked.

"Had to," I said. I know it was a short answer, but it was that simple.

"That's it?" Mom persisted.

"Yup."

"What do you think your father will say?" she wondered.

I gave that a little bit of thought before I replied. "'How'd she handle?' I hope."

I didn't have to wait long to find out what Dad had to say. Mom dragged me to the hospital. She had a firm hand on my neck as she steered me down a long white hall. Marty, Mark, and Leon marched behind us.

When we got to Dad's room, I said to her, "I want to go in alone."

Mom understood. She always did. She nodded and opened the door for me.

As I went in, I heard Mark say, "Give me a choice, I'd take the bear cave."

Well, Dad was back in his traction. I guess he must have pulled everything off to go to the window. But he was lying there smoking a smelly old cigar. The smoke hung like a cloud around his head. He was wearing his poker face.

I just looked him in the eye and said, "Dad, I think you've got some explaining to do."

Outside in the hall, Marty told me later, he was worried because it was so quiet. Mark was sure that was because Dad had killed me.

But he hadn't. We were just having a long-overdue talk.

I said, "Work hard, don't be afraid of anything,

always tell the truth. Is that right, Dad?" See, he hadn't been living up to his own rules.

When he answered, Dad's voice was icy calm. "I'm not going to be in this hospital bed forever, son. Then what?"

That was scary. I felt a chill run up my spine. But if he could keep his poker face, so could I. After all, I was his son. So I went on as cool as I could. "Well, I guess I'll probably go one on one with the belt. But that's later. What I'm askin' now is for you to cut Marty and Mark loose."

Dad looked a little puzzled. So I said, "Let them go finish the film."

"Are you telling me what to do?" Dad growled.

I looked into his eyes, and all my anger went away. "No, Dad. I'm asking you."

His eyes never left mine. Dad took the wet cigar stub out of his mouth and slowly ground it out in an ashtray by the bed. He shook his head a little, like he just couldn't believe what he was hearing, or what he'd seen. Then Dad cleared his throat. "So, Marshall, how'd she handle?"

I had to smile. I forgave him. I just walked right over, put my head on his chest, and hugged him tight.

Dad lifted his hands like he was going to hug me, too. But, you know, Dad was really kind of shy. He didn't like to do stuff like that. So his big hands just hung in the air above my back for the longest time. Then they floated down.

Until just now, I never told anybody what happened that day between Dad and me. I don't think they would have believed me anyway. Marty and Mark were astonished that I was still alive, and I didn't even get whupped.

CHAPTER
14

The great day finally came. We'd put up posters and sold tickets to the premiere of our movie. We had a pretty good crowd in the school gym that night.

On a big white screen I saw that giant gator skimming through the water right behind me. To tell the truth, I had no idea he was that big.

Suddenly the camera spun crazily. You could see trees and Marty's panicked face, and a brief, cockeyed view of Mark pulling himself into the boat. The gator's flashing eyes glared into the lens. We had him! As sure as if we'd shot him, like old Ernie-Bob Hemingway.

I took a quick look at our audience. Mom sat between Leon and Bud from the camera store. Bud muttered to Marty, "Had to drive all the way to Little Rock myself to get the film. Only had time to splice the reels together."

Donna Jo Stewart looked away from the screen and gave Marty the once-over. He was nervous enough to look cute. Their eyes met, and she smiled. It was a nice smile. Marty's face was about as red as it had been up in the cave of bears.

Not everybody loved the movie. Some people didn't. Some didn't care much either way. They laughed at the sight of Mark and his cut butt.

Some of the footage was bad. That Mexican wolf was overexposed. We had more shots of dust than mustangs in the great desert stampede.

D. C. and his buddies made rude noises and shouted out snide remarks like "Loser film, man!" and "Snoozer."

One old guy fell asleep.

The scene changed to the dark shape of the cave of bears looming in the snowy landscape. There was a quick jostled shot of the cave floor writhing with rattlers.

I felt a stab of fear again. I could hear 'em.

Then there were quick shots of huge dark shapes

rising in the dim cave. And suddenly something flashed straight at the camera. A huge bear paw smacked into the lens! The picture spun like a downed plane.

I thought the movie was over then. We broke the camera. But something wonderful happened! The Arriflex kept running!

For a brief moment, there we were: sideways on the screen, eyes poppin', jaws dropped as we stared straight into the lens. Then the screen was speckled with yellow dots. The countdown numbers of leader tape appeared. The film flapped through the projector gate and the screen went white.

I guess the audience didn't expect that kind of ending. There was a stunned silence. The lights came up. There was a smattering of polite applause.

D. C.'s nasal whine carried over the other sounds. "Stouffer, you should have paid *me* to sit through this," he drawled.

Everyone stopped clapping. There was a brief, awkward silence. And from the back of the room there was one loud, slow clap. Then another and another.

The whole town turned to see Dad. He was leaning on crutches, and he was applauding his boys.

With tears in her eyes, Mom joined him. Then Leon, the Stewart sisters, and Bud, and it slowly built until a good many people were clapping. The sound filled the gym.

But D. C., with Julie Ann on his arm and followed by his goon squad, strode up to me and my brothers. "We want our money back," he demanded.

Now, Marty was just about a heartbeat away from tearing that old boy's arm off and beating him over the head with it. But it was Dad's voice that cut through the tension. "You saw a pretty good show for your money," he said.

D. C. thought he was tough, but he jumped a little.

Dad took a ten-dollar bill from his wallet. "My treat," he said.

I gasped. It was amazing enough that he had shown up at all, much less applauded. But for Dad to pry open his wallet and hand his hard-earned money over to D. C. like that was nothing short of a miracle. I looked up, half-expecting to see my guardian angel laughing above me. But all I saw was the gym ceiling.

Donna Jo Stewart said, "Take the money and get out of here, you big dumb animal."

D. C. blushed as red as a peach. Everybody stared at him and his buddies. They just walked away, without Dad's money.

Donna Jo said, "We thought it was good. A little short, but good."

Her sister, Tanna, smiled. "It was brilliant!"

The three of us felt like the kings of creation. Marty got excited. "We'll finish the film! We'll sell it to TV, maybe get somebody famous to narrate it!" The fire was back in his eyes.

"We'll get Robert Redford," Mark chimed in.

"Groovy!" the Stewart sisters cooed together.

I could tell that Marty and Mark felt famous already. Marty was already arranging his collection of Emmies and a couple of Oscars on his big Hollywood mantel.

I couldn't blame him. It was a wonderful night. But the most wonderful thing of all was yet to come: Dad smiled.

Well, you know, Marty wasn't really crazy after all. He went on to shoot over a million feet of the best American wildlife footage ever. His first movie, *The Predators*, narrated by Robert Redford, aired on April 6, 1977, on the NBC network.

Marty went on to produce and host a successful

nature television series. Mark became one of the foremost wildlife filmmakers in the world. I myself recently completed a documentary about endangered snails. It's safer than bears! But I'm looking for bigger game now.

And, oh yeah, Mom spent two glorious weeks on the beaches of Hawaii. Dad scoured the island for car parts.